HISTORY
IN YOUR
HAND

HISTORY IN YOUR HAND

Fifty Years of the Manuscript Society

JOHN M. TAYLOR

Foreword by
John D. Haskell

*Sponsored by
the Manuscript Society*

Westport, Connecticut
London

Library of Congress Cataloging-in-Publication Data

Taylor, John M., 1930–
 History in your hand : fifty years of the Manuscript Society /
John M. Taylor ; foreword by John D. Haskell.
  p. cm.
 Includes bibliographical references (p.) and index.
 ISBN 0–275–95918–X (alk. paper)
 1. Manuscript Society (U.S.)—History. 2. Manuscripts—Societies,
etc.—History. I. Title.
 Z108.T38 1997
 091′.06′073—dc21   96–54066

British Library Cataloguing in Publication Data is available.

Library of Congress Catalog Card Number: 96–54066
ISBN: 0–275–95918–X

First published in 1997

Praeger Publishers, 88 Post Road West, Westport, CT 06881
An imprint of Greenwood Publishing Group, Inc.

Printed in the United States of America

The paper used in this book complies with the
Permanent Paper Standard issued by the National
Information Standards Organization (Z39.48–1984).

10 9 8 7 6 5 4 3 2 1

Contents

Foreword

A half century, 1948–97, and what a half century it has been! These five decades saw three wars involving the United States, 10 presidents and a presidential assassination, a moon landing, the eradication of many childhood diseases, another San Francisco earthquake, domestic terrorism, and the dawn of the age of cyberspace. Through all of this, a small international organization devoted to the collection, preservation, and enjoyment of autographs and manuscripts was born, has matured, and today flourishes as the senior organization of its kind in the world.

The 15 collectors who met at the University Club in Chicago on the third day of 1948 to found the National Society of Autograph Collectors (which became the Manuscript Society in 1953) sowed the seeds of a thriving organization that today boasts some 1,800 members; it also publishes a respected quarterly journal, *Manuscripts*, and, since 1980, an informative quarterly newsletter.

Annual meetings, the first of which was held at the University of Michigan in Ann Arbor in May 1948 with some 75 persons in attendance, have continued without interruption. Gatherings have been held in 22 states, the District of Columbia, and four foreign locations. At these meetings Society members have been addressed by such notables as Lewis Mumford, Catherine Drinker Bowen, Bruce Catton, and Coretta Scott King. They have had the opportunity to view some of the most important manuscripts of the Western world, in repositories throughout North America and abroad. Equally important, they have had the opportunity to examine and admire prize items from the collections of fellow members!

John M. Taylor, a former Society president and the author of numerous other books in history and biography, has produced an eminently readable and comprehensive history of the Society's first 50 years, and of the world of autographs during that period. *History in Your Hand* covers a wide spectrum of issues, from price escalation to the Autopen, from remarkable acts of altruism by Society members to the sinister forgeries of Mark Hofmann. The book describes in interesting detail the court cases in which the Society has defended autograph owners against attempts by government authorities to replevin "lost" manuscripts.

This book has benefited immensely from repeated readings by Priscilla Taylor, editor of Phi Beta Kappa's *Key Reporter* and an associate editor of the *New York Public Library Writer's Guide to Style and Usage*. The Society is grateful for her assistance.

This fine narrative will serve many generations as a comprehensive account of the early years of the foremost organization devoted to the collection and preservation of *History in Your Hand*.

John D. Haskell
Williamsburg, Virginia
August 1996

Acknowledgments

The Manuscript Society gratefully acknowledges the financial support of the following members and friends, whose contributions made this book possible:

PATRONS

William R. and Monique Coleman

Ceci and John H. Keck

Herbert E. and Angelika Klingelhofer

Richard Maass

Anthony Mourek

David R. Smith

SUBSCRIBERS

Charles and Lois Apfelbaum

Charles I. Bernold

Norman F. Boas

Francis A. Brennan

Ira Brilliant

Stephen W. Bumball

Syd Cauveren

David R. Chesnutt

H. Bart Cox

J. Leonard Diamond

Duane Norman Diedrich

Ray Dubberke

Dorothy Eaton

Ernest C. Fackler

Joseph E. Fields

Everett Fisher

John H. Freund

Ira M. Goldberg

Mrs. S. Howard Goldman

Mr. and Mrs. Harry E. Gould Jr.

Gary Grossman

H. De Forest Hardinge

John D. Haskell Jr.

Michael and Donna Hecht

James D. and Renette Hier

Robert R. Hudson

Christopher C. Jaeckel

Alvin R. and Marjory Kantor

Shinaan Krakowsky

Susan Coblentz Lane

H. Jack Lang

Walter G. Langlois

Kenneth R. Laurence

David and Sondra Light

Paul V. Lutz

Dolly Maass

Father Bradley McCormick

Robert McCown

Barbara McCrimmon

Alphonse A. Maffeo

Frank Mattson

Ivo Meisner

Sanford and Patricia Mock

Earl Moore

Robert Moore

Scott J. Mubarak

Kenneth Nebenzahl

Barbara Ogilvie

Thomas J. O'Neill

Cordelia and Tom Platt

Russell A. Price

John M. Reznikoff

Brian J. Richter

Leon Robbin

Herbert and Aphrodite Rubin

Joseph Rubinfine

Helen and George Sanders

Steven Schiffer

Ken Schwartz

Benjamin Shapell

L. Dennis Shapiro

Milton R. Slater

Albert H. Small

Murray J. and Dinah Smith

R. M. Smythe & Co.

J. Humbert Tinsman Jr.

Tollett and Harman Autographs

Scott R. Trepel

Virginia Polytechnic Institute Libraries

Peggy West

Glen N. Wiche

James A. Wilson

Laetitia Yeandle

David Zucker, Jerry Zucker, and
  Ken Ziffren

CHAPTER 1

A Meeting in Chicago

Nineteen forty-eight was an eventful year. In May, the United States recognized the newly created state of Israel. In June, Soviet authorities initiated the blockade of West Berlin that led the United States to respond with an airlift of food and supplies. In September, a crowd of dignitaries dedicated New York City's Idlewild Airport, then the largest in the world.

In the same year, novelist James Gould Cozzens won the Pulitzer Prize for *Guard of Honor*, a story of racism on a U.S. air base. Norman Mailer published *The Naked and the Dead*. Rodgers and Hammerstein's *South Pacific* was the toast of Broadway. Joe Louis was heavyweight champion of the world, and the Cleveland Indians were about to defeat the Boston Braves in the World Series. Although 1948 was a presidential election year, interest in politics was minimal. Everyone knew that Governor Thomas E. Dewey of New York would easily defeat the unpopular incumbent president, Harry S. Truman.

Largely unnoticed was a meeting held at the University Club in Chicago on January 3, 1948. There, a group of 15 collectors formally launched the National Society of Autograph Collectors (NSAC), the first such organization in the world. The *New York Times* reported briefly that the new organization would hold a general meeting at the University of Michigan in May. A longer article in the *New York Sun* quoted the NSAC's aims as "to encourage the meeting of autograph collectors, to stimulate and aid them in their various collecting specialties, to facilitate the exchange of information and knowledge among collectors and scholars." Provisional president of the Society was obstetrician Joseph E. Fields of Joliet, Illinois, whom the *Sun* called "an outstanding collector [and] one of the moving spirits behind the organization."[1]

The idea of an organization for autograph collectors was not new. Forest H. Sweet, who, with his father, ran an autograph dealership in Battle Creek, Michigan, recalled that one of his customers had raised the subject of such an organization before World War II. On the East Coast, Alexander Armour, a prominent collector, had attempted unsuccessfully to drum up interest in a national society. Another collector, Herbert Klingelhofer, a dentist in Washington, D.C., recalls once asking a New York City dealer, Thomas F. Madigan, how he might get in touch with fellow collectors. Madigan replied that there was no "ready path" to other collectors. There ought to be an autograph society, he mused, "but I never heard of one."[2] This was in about 1936.

It was the bluff and outspoken Sweet who, in the autumn of 1947, became the catalyst in the successful drive for a national organization. It all began with a football game. Joe Fields was eager to obtain tickets for some friends to a sold-out game between the Michigan and Minnesota university teams. When he mentioned his need to Sweet, the dealer told him that one of his customers, Allyn Ford, had the right connections, and, sure enough, Ford came up with tickets. Sweet wrote to Fields before the game, urging him to meet with Ford to consider a collectors organization. "If you two alone form it," he wrote, "I know a dozen or 20 who will instantly apply for membership." Tongue firmly in cheek, Sweet added, "There won't be any duties for either of you until you hold the first annual meeting, and by that time you will have enough members so you can wish all the work onto them."[3]

Ford did not attend the football game, but he and Fields began corresponding on the possibility of a national organization of autograph collectors. Their personal collecting interests proved a bond. Fields specialized in the American Revolution, while Ford—president of a company whose laundry products included "Mrs. Stewart's Bluing"—had eclectic collecting interests.

Sweet continued to act as an intermediary. Why not bring in Ralph Newman of the Abraham Lincoln Book Shop? Fields arranged an organizational meeting at Newman's shop, then located on North Michigan Avenue, for October 15, 1947. The 10 people there included, in addition to Sweet and Fields, two prominent Civil War historians, Paul M. Angle and E. B. "Pete" Long. In Sweet's jocular recollection,

Otto Eisenschiml wanted [the Society] started as a Chicago local, like the . . . Civil War Round Table. [Dr. Max] Thorek threatened to put back Otto's gall bladder if he didn't stop opposing. Dick Lederer more than any other person—being a New Yorker and being an extrovert—really congealed the diverse opinions into a singular one. Ralph [Newman] . . . wrote the aims. Paul [Angle] cut them down.[4]

The consensus was that the organization should be national in scope, should have a journal, and should meet annually. Six hundred dollars was pledged toward expenses. All involved assumed that the new organization would be a collectors group; the role to be played by dealers and archivists was unspecified. For the moment, the talk was of formally launching the Society early in 1948, and of holding a national meeting later that year.

After considerable networking by the preparatory committee, a second meeting was held in Chicago on November 13. Allyn Ford arranged to attend. Neither Sweet nor Fields had yet met Ford, but the man from Minneapolis caught their attention at the railroad station by waving a bottle of his product, Mrs. Stewart's Bluing! The meeting itself drew 16 collectors from three states. There was a spirited discussion as to what type of organization they had in mind. Ralph Newman, like Eisenschiml, favored a local organization, along the lines of a Civil War Round Table. Max Thorek argued vigorously for a national group, which someone else dismissed as "a lonely hearts club for autograph collectors." In a key decision, those in favor of a national organization carried the day. The result was the formal launching of the National Society of Autograph Collectors on January 3, 1948.

Who was the first autograph collector? No one knows, although *Antiquarian Bookman* once put in a whimsical claim for St. Paul, citing the second Epistle to Timothy (4:13), "When you come, bring . . . the books and above all the parchments."[5]

The more recent collecting of important autographs had its origins in about the sixteenth century, with the spread of the printed word, especially in Germany. From the printed word it was but a short step to the manuscript behind the book. The German poet Goethe once boasted of his collection of autographs, adding, "I . . . often take occasion to examine and reflect upon them."[6]

Autograph collecting did not catch on in the United States until the early decades of the nineteenth century. Attempts at that time to preserve the correspondence of leaders of the American Revolution led to collecting specialties in U.S. presidents, Signers of the Declaration of Independence, and prominent authors. The first important collector of American autographs may have been the Reverend William B. Sprague, a Presbyterian clergyman. As a young man Sprague served as tutor in the Virginia home of Major Lawrence Lewis, a nephew of George Washington. Bushrod Washington, a Supreme Court justice and a nephew of the first president, allowed Sprague to extract any letter he desired from Washington's correspondence, as long as he left a copy in its place, and Sprague thus acquired about 1,500 Washington items. Sprague is generally credited with the idea of forming sets of the Signers of the Declaration of Independence; at one time his collection included three such sets.[7]

The greatest American collector of the nineteenth century, and probably of all time, was the financier J. Pierpont Morgan. Although his primary interest was in rare books, the line between an ancient volume and a manuscript is often blurred, and this was certainly so for Morgan. At one time his collection included two Gutenberg Bibles, Dickens's original manuscript of *A Christmas Carol*, and the only known manuscript fragment from Milton's *Paradise Lost*. An awestruck correspondent from *The Times* of London reported in 1908:

I have entered the most carefully guarded treasurehouse in the world, and nothing in it has been hidden from me. Mr. J. Pierpont Morgan is probably the greatest collector of things splendid and beautiful and rare who has ever lived.[8]

The later collectors who banded to form the National Society of Autograph Collectors were hardly in Morgan's class financially. Moreover, they faced some unusual problems, some of them unique to the autograph world. Autograph collectors are not to be compared with other hobbyists, not even most philatelists. The collecting of autographs and manuscripts is usually a very private avocation, and it has long been a field dominated by men. If a collector shares one of his gems, it is usually with a collector friend or two, over brandy and cigars.

Many collectors are protective about their fields of interest, some viewing their peers as competitors rather than as kindred spirits. Dealers, for their part, go to extraordinary measures to maintain a special relationship with favored, wealthy clients. Would it be possible to form a workable national organization from such a group of prima donnas?

President Fields's report on the January 3 preparatory meeting circulated among collectors in the month that followed. A second circular announced the first Executive Committee: Alexander Armour of Princeton, New Jersey; Allyn Ford of Minneapolis; Colonel Roy G. Fitzgerald of Dayton, Ohio; Richard M. Lederer of New York; and five men from the Chicago area: Robert L. Huttner, Dr. C. W. Olsen, Colonel William Herzog, Foreman Lebold, and Dr. Max Thorek. The secretary, Elaine Madlener, was the sole woman on the committee. The first committee thus had a strongly male and midwestern flavor.

Fields, in a February circular, advised the collector community that the NSAC planned to incorporate as a nonprofit institution in Illinois. Dues were set at $5 for regular members, $25 for contributing members, and $100 for sustaining members. At the January 3 meeting the board agreed that all members who enrolled during the first two years would be regarded as charter members.[9] The controversial portion of Fields's report concerned membership and objectives:

All the members were of the opinion that this society must be of, by, and for the collectors. We welcome . . . allied collectors whose field overlaps into the autograph and manuscript field. I refer to the book and stamp collector whose interests carry him into autographs. It was likewise agreed that dealers, librarians, curators, archivists, and professionals of all kinds should be admitted but should not hold office. . . . All traces of commercialism must be kept out.[10]

Some of this language would later haunt the Society, but for the moment the focus was on the meeting to be held at the University of Michigan's Clements Library, and on recruitment of new members. Richard Maass wrote from New York that the collectors he had contacted were enthusiastic about the proposed organization. Allyn Ford thought it remarkable that he was unearthing fellow collectors in his own backyard. "Here in the Twin Cities, I thought I was the only collector of consequence," Ford wrote to Philadelphia dealer Charles Sessler, "but since talking to Dr. Fields I have heard of two in St. Paul, and we are planning to get together in the near future."[11]

A board meeting at the Chicago Historical Society in March focused on the Society's proposed journal. E. B. Long, whose *The Civil War Day by Day* would later become a vital tool for Civil War researchers, volunteered to launch it. Meanwhile, reports on the initial membership drive were highly encouraging. Richard Lederer wrote to California collector Justin "Jack" Turner that paid membership had reached 170 and that a regional chapter was being organized in New York City. "Joe Fields, Allyn Ford and Forest Sweet are doing a grand job," he wrote, "and as a result we are making great headway."[12]

The initial reaction of the dealer community to the NSAC was mixed. Several dealers expressed support, but on January 19, 1948, Mary Benjamin, the New York dealer who published *The Collector*, wrote to Fields that she had concluded "that it is not wise for me to make any announcement whatsoever about the autograph association until your plans are more settled."[13] Fields passed the letter along to his colleagues with a dismissive note. Allyn Ford wrote to Fields, "When you consider that Rosenbach and Bloomfield are with us, I don't think we need worry about Mary, and the other people that she is trying to influence."[14]

Mary Benjamin was not the only person in the small dealer community who harbored misgivings about a national organization of collectors along the lines spelled out in Chicago. Some felt that the NSAC's exclusion of dealers from its board was evidence of discrimination. Others wondered whether NSAC-inspired rapport among collectors might not endanger their relationships with special clients. Publicity-shy collectors harbored doubts regarding NSAC assurances that they could enroll on a secret, unpublished membership list. Sol Malkin, publisher of *Antiquarian Bookman*, thought this provision for anonymity ridiculous. Urging that the Society eschew secrecy, Malkin wrote to Forest Sweet that membership in a group entailed certain obligations. "If someone is unwilling to [identify himself], you have the genesis of a 'secret' society."[15]

On March 5, 1948, six East Coast dealers, unhappy with the NSAC, sent a joint letter to Fields reporting on a meeting they had held in New York City in late February:

All the dealers present, with a single exception [not identified], felt that the NSAC press release [of February 23] required clarification. It was felt that the NSAC proposed an unnecessary discrimination against dealers, librarians and other professional collectors who were offered Class B memberships without the rights and privileges of other members.

As for membership lists, "The dealers were of the opinion that membership lists would become known to most members, including dealers, and it would therefore be a sound policy for the NSAC to institute from the very beginning the policy of publishing names."[16] Gordon Banks, one of the dealers present, wrote to Fields privately, characterizing the meeting as "a rather boisterous two hours." He thought that the dealers definitely felt left out, but assured Fields that they had no great interest in holding office, beyond perhaps having one position on the board.[17]

Fields attempted to mediate the dispute. In a four-page, single-spaced letter to Mary Benjamin, he cited the NSAC's rapidly expanding membership as evidence that the Society was firmly established. He sought to deal with the apprehension many dealers felt about turning over their mailing lists to any organization. Any list submitted to the Society in confidence, Fields wrote, would be treated as confidential and dealt with by a membership committee composed of collectors only. As for dealers on the board,

I am greatly disturbed that you feel we have discriminated against the dealers by putting them in a separate class. . . . Such a ruling was by the common consent of the directors on January 3. This rule is subject to change. . . . It was done to protect the members from overcommercialism and to protect the dealers themselves.[18]

In early April, Mary Benjamin wrote to Fields in a conciliatory vein: "I flatter myself that, when THE COLLECTOR carries the article on the new Society, a number of [my customers] will be stirred into joining."[19]

The first of what were to become annual meetings of the NSAC was held at the University of Michigan's Clements Library on May 17–18, 1948. Seventy-nine members attended what President Fields called the largest gathering of autograph collectors ever held. A newspaper reporter detected a slightly elitist tone:

The country's serious autograph collectors—not to be confused with the people who extort scrawled signatures from celebrities—are banding together for the first time this month to form a national organization. . . .

Serious collectors are generally considered to be those who acquire fifty autographs or more of a collated nature. . . . Totaling not more than 3,000 persons in the United States, the serious collectors will have their first opportunity to find kindred souls in large numbers at the first meeting of the National Society of Autograph Collectors.[20]

The centerpiece of the meeting was an exhibition of members' autographs. President Fields showed off his collection of Signers of the Declaration. Visitors admired a 1782 Washington letter, directing that a strict guard be placed over arms and munitions surrendered by Cornwallis at Yorktown. In an autographed letter signed (ALS), Thomas Jefferson viewed with alarm the growing power of the Supreme Court, declaring that "the germ of dissolution of our Federal government is in the constitution of our Federal judiciary." Lincoln autographs on display included a letter to the governor of Pennsylvania, signed during the Battle of Gettysburg, levying an additional draft of men from that state.[21]

In the formal proceedings, University of Michigan president Alexander G. Ruthven and Clements Library director Randolph Adams welcomed the Society to the campus. A banquet that evening included a panel discussion on "The Role of the Collector." At the business meeting the following day, the Society adopted a constitution that provided for the election of officers and a 15-person board of directors. Madlener, the secretary, reported that membership had reached 250; E. B. Long, the journal editor, reported that he was getting a good response to a letter asking for contributions on behalf of the journal, but that no date for the first issue had yet been set.

The provisional officers and directors, led by Fields, were permanently elected. Recognizing that the first board had been heavily weighted with persons from the Chicago area, directors from the two coasts were added.

Among them, Justin Turner of Los Angeles and Alexander Armour of Princeton, New Jersey, would be active for many years.

The board meeting on May 18 was concerned primarily with the proposed journal. The Society had only a few hundred dollars in the bank, and a quarterly publication loomed as a major undertaking. Gordon Banks proposed that the Society commit itself to a single issue in 1948 and work its way up to a quarterly schedule. The board concurred and engaged Chicago printer Norman Forgue to produce 1,500 copies of the *Autograph Collectors' Journal*.

At the close of the meeting, President Fields reflected on the events of the past few months:

> Six short months ago the National Society of Autograph Collectors was a dream in the minds of a few collectors. . . . Until the formation of the NSAC no organization had ever existed for those interested in autographs and manuscript material. There was no outlet for their inspirations and ideas. . . .
>
> It was with a twofold purpose that the NSAC was organized: first, to revive the spirit of comradeship among collectors, and, second, to disseminate information and knowledge among collectors and scholars.[22]

At last, American autograph collectors had an organization to call their own. The most enthusiastic response to the new society came from the trade weekly *Antiquarian Bookman*, whose proprietor, Sol Malkin, would prove a faithful supporter of the NSAC and its successor, the Manuscript Society, over the years. Malkin editorialized in his publication on May 29, 1948, that "members of the [book] trade who are at all interested in autographs and have not yet joined the NSAC are urged to do so."

CHAPTER 2

Ford's Theatre and Other Capers

Who were the autograph collectors of the 1950s? Libraries had long been repositories for autographs; indeed, they had traditionally been the institutions through which historical documents had been preserved. Private collectors were comparatively few in number, but they shared certain characteristics:

- They were likely to be college graduates with an interest in history.
- With a few exceptions, they were financially well off without qualifying as "rich." An auction house could realize more from the sale of a single painting than from an entire sale of books or autographs.

Forest Sweet articulated a common view in a letter to Joe Fields in 1956.

Autographs are really the poor man's . . . field [for] collecting unique items. He can't do it in stamps, coins, paintings, silver, china, furniture, or anything else I can think of. In letters he can—my collector of Memphis [material], or Buffalo Bill or Winfield Scott . . . gets *unique* items which are just as important to him as a [much rarer autograph] is to you.[1]

Collectors tended to take one of two approaches to collecting, though a degree of overlap was common. One was to specialize in a period or subject. Although by far the largest number of respondents to a survey of NSAC members in the early 1960s listed categories such as the American Revolution, Signers of the Declaration of Independence, the Civil War, and broader fields such as literature and music, among the less common categories listed were account books, anti-Masonic material, bastards, dance, evolution, the Inquisition, and Samoa.

A second approach was to specialize in material of specific individuals. Sought-after autographs of the 1950s included those of Washington, Franklin, Lincoln, Napoleon, and Poe.

Whichever approach or combination of approaches was chosen, a collector was usually alert to collateral material relating to the subject. A collector of Civil War military items often sought out material of prominent political and literary figures of the period as well. The collector of Benjamin Franklin letters was probably interested also in letters of his descendants and letters written *to* Ben. Then as now, except for a few notable rarities, fine content was prized above all else.

The early members of the NSAC—men like Alexander Armour, Otto Fischer, William Herzog, Foreman Lebold, Victor Hugo Paltsits, and Frank Pleadwell—may or may not have been more virtuous and better looking than their counterparts today. But circumstances, most notably the absence of a broadly based autograph "market," made for a good deal of friendly rapport. As for acquisitions, an autograph was rarely purchased as a "good investment," to be shopped from one auction house to another until it met its reserve and turned a profit. Instead, there was considerable trading among collectors, who were sensitive to the special wants of their colleagues.

Unlike many artifacts of the famous, every autograph is unique, and its authenticity can usually be established beyond reasonable doubt. Not so with other memorabilia. The Louisa May Alcott scholar Madeleine Stern tells how she and her business partner, Leona Rostenberg, were visiting a house in which the Alcotts had lived when they were shown a large copper teakettle that was said to be one that Alcott had taken to Washington when she was a nurse in the Civil War. Stern recalls:

> The same day I paid a visit to the Concord Antiquarian Society nearby where, among other relics, I was shown a slightly smaller copper teakettle. "This," the curator informed me with pride, "is the teakettle Louisa took with her to Washington when she was a nurse in the Civil War." Horrified, I exclaimed, "But they showed me the teakettle she took to Washington in the Orchard House!" The curator's reply was a cautionary warning for all time. With a slight frown and a shrug of annoyance she said, "Did they? We had an understanding that *this* year it was to be *our* teakettle."[2]

The sociologist Si Kahn, writing on organizations, notes that many start from a base sufficiently small "that the leaders can do the necessary work on a volunteer basis. But then the organization starts growing. It's no longer a group of friends who get together once a week."[3] The roots of the NSAC were in Chicago, but the meeting at Ann Arbor had turned it into a national organization. Growth was rapid but helter-skelter. Local chapters sprang up in New York City and Los Angeles. Membership reflected the early spurt characteristic of new organizations.

The evolution of an organization is reflected to some degree in its constitution, especially in the changes that are required over the years. The first constitution of the NSAC was a short and general document of only eight articles. Anyone "in sympathy with the objects of the Society" was eligible for membership. Authority was vested in a 15-person board of directors, who served a three-year term and were responsible for electing the officers. The idea of barring dealers from board membership was quietly scrapped.

The only Society activity addressed in the constitution was the annual meeting, which, the document specified, could not be held in the same city for two successive years. Article VIII dealt with local chapters—a reminder of the importance that the Society's founders attached to these regional groups. As few as five members could form a chapter, with the approval of the board of directors.[4] President Fields wrote in a 1949 article for *Antiquarian Bookman*:

One of the most important activities of the Society has been in the field of local chapters. At present there are chapters in New York, Minneapolis–St. Paul, and Los Angeles. A chapter is in the process of formation in the San Francisco area.[5]

By far the most vigorous chapter was that in the New York area. This is hardly surprising, for New York represented the greatest concentration of collectors and dealers in the country, including prominent NSAC members such as Richard Lederer, Alexander Armour, Richard Maass, and Nat Stein. As early as April 1948, Lederer wrote to Fields, "Friday's meeting was a huge success, with 24 in attendance. . . . Two residents of Nutley, N.J., not known to each other before, went home together, likewise two from Bronxville."[6] More than a year later, there was press coverage of a dinner meeting at which Frederick B. Adams, director of the Morgan Library, discussed J. Pierpont Morgan's autograph collection. At subsequent chapter meetings the Reverend Cornelius Greenway discussed his collection of inscribed photographs, Van Dyk MacBride spoke on autographs and philately, and Edward Marsh lectured on preservation.

By 1950 the New York chapter had hosted no fewer than 13 dinner meetings, with attendance as high as 60 persons. The press of that day attempted to cover the activities of prominent collector organizations, and in November 1950 the *New York World Telegram and Sun* summarized a talk by Arthur Swann of Parke-Bernet Galleries about the five copies of the Gettysburg Address in Lincoln's hand. Most of Swann's remarks concerned the fair copy that Lincoln gave Colonel Alexander Bliss to have auctioned off for the benefit of Union casualties and their families. According to Swann, the Bliss family later invited the pioneer dealer Thomas Madigan to bid for the document. During negotiations, Madigan examined portions of it with a pocket magnifying glass. Mrs. Bliss interpreted his action as reflecting on the authenticity of the manuscript and subsequently refused to part with it![7]

Outside New York, the progress of local chapters was slow. Allyn Ford wrote to Fields of a meeting of the Twin Cities chapter that had drawn only seven attendees; Ford was not sure that a chapter could flourish there even if book collectors were included.[8] The Los Angeles area, however, appeared promising. Board member Jack Turner took charge, and by the fall of 1949 meetings in the Los Angeles area were well attended.

So active were the New York members of the Society that they found time to arrange an autograph exhibit—featuring members of New York University's hall of fame—at the National Antiques Show in Madison Square Garden a month before the May 1949 annual meeting.

Nat Stein, one of the exhibitors, recounted two contrasting reactions to the NSAC exhibit. At one time he noticed two black women hovering around a display case containing Lincoln material. When Nat asked if he could be of any assistance, the younger woman somewhat nervously asked whether it might be possible for the case to be opened, and her elderly mother allowed to touch a document in Lincoln's hand. Ignoring all security rules, Stein opened the case and granted his visitors' wish.

The exhibit drew a different reaction from a couple from Texas who sauntered over after viewing the antiques. The Texan was spellbound by the autograph exhibit, and, reaching for his checkbook, offered to buy "the whole shebang." To his wife's plea that there were other antiques in the show he replied, "That's junk; this is the real thing!"[9]

Close on the heels of the Madison Square Garden exhibition came the annual meeting at Princeton, New Jersey. The theme there was cooperation, and a succession of speakers supported interaction, as opposed to competition, among collectors, dealers, and archivists. Forest Sweet spoke on behalf of the dealer community, Leon de Valinger for the Delaware state archives, and Lyman H. Butterfield on behalf of the Papers of Thomas Jefferson. If some of the speeches tended to be banal, the format nevertheless represented an effort by the NSAC to become more inclusive. And some of the presentations were provocative. Butterfield took on the perennial issue of whether publication of a letter reduces its value. He did not believe that it did and cited his own experience in editing the papers of Benjamin Rush:

The long and splendid series of John Adams letters to Rush, gathered in the first series of Col. Biddle's volume of *Old Family Letters* in 1892, [sold at auction] at uniformly high prices. On an average, they certainly brought more than stray Adams letters [had brought] in previous years. As for the Rush autographs, those that brought much the highest prices were precisely the ones that had been printed by Col. Biddle in his *Old Family Letters*.[10]

The banquet speaker, David Mearns of the Library of Congress, shared some historical anecdotes. He talked about the superintendent of printing in the Lincoln administration, whose name he never mentioned, who had cut up the manuscript of Lincoln's last message to Congress, distributing scraps to friends much as Jared Sparks had emasculated Washington's draft farewell address. In a more positive vein, Mearns recalled his own visit to the White House, to consult the country's most famous bibliophile, Franklin D. Roosevelt.

He was in [the White House library] when I arrived, and as a preliminary to the business, he displayed his treasures with the infectious enthusiasm and startling animation which were so notably his. Seated in a wheel chair, with a frame of light metal, he would whisk himself from shelf to shelf and proudly exhibit the books which held a special interest for him. Most of them were the work of moderns and most of them were gaily inscribed. He read the inscriptions aloud and chuckled over them.[11]

The Princeton meeting marked the first time that the Society had sponsored an auction in order to raise funds. At Princeton, a checkbook used by Stonewall Jackson went for $105, while a Lincoln document brought $85. The sale netted a total of $1,047, most of which was earmarked for the journal.

The most ambitious project in the early years of the NSAC was the launching of a quarterly journal. There was a great deal of enthusiasm for the enterprise, because many of the members were experts on some historic figure or some aspect of autograph collecting and were eager to put their views on paper. The only thing missing had been a publication devoted to autographs.

E. B. Long had accepted the unpaid editorship of the *Autograph Collectors' Journal*, with a proviso that he could commit himself only for the first two issues. The first issue appeared in October 1948, in a 32-page format.

It contained five articles, the lead article by Victor Hugo Paltsits on a spurious John Hancock document that purported to be George Washington's commission as commanding general of the colonial armies. Paltsits concluded that it was a nineteenth-century forgery. The first issue of the journal was an artistic success but an expensive one, for there were few advertisements. (Of the handful of dealers who purchased ads, only one—Maggs Brothers, Ltd., of London—is still in operation today.)

The journal's news section reported this story from the nation's capital:

> Fire in a Washington stable last New Year's Eve revealed a treasure trove of colonial historical documents, including a Washington letter. Library of Congress manuscript specialists have been busy trying to catalogue and restore checks, letters and documents found in the rubbish from the fire. . . . The documents were the papers of Samuel Galloway, who lived in Maryland. The stable was owned by a Galloway descendant.[12]

The January 1949 issue followed much the same format; it led with an article by Joseph Fields on the various copies of General Robert E. Lee's famous General Order No. 9. The issue also contained some book reviews and news from the chapters in New York and Minneapolis. Among the news notes was an interesting offer from an anonymous collector, who said that he had a note by General Henry W. Halleck relating to a soldier named Harris who appeared to have been pardoned by Lincoln. He offered to provide the Halleck note gratis to whoever might have the Lincoln pardon.

Colton Storm succeeded Long as editor that spring, and his first issue consisted almost exclusively of papers delivered at the Princeton meeting. The July 1949 issue, however, returned to the earlier, varied format. Howard Peckham contributed an offbeat article on the autographs of illiterates, citing persons of historical importance—including Chief Pontiac, Dred Scott, and the founder of the Shakers, Ann Lee—who could only make their mark.

The position of journal editor was demanding, and, after putting out two issues in 1949, Storm resigned; his position was taken by George H. Crosbie Jr., a New York collector with experience in editing a business newsletter.

The Society's third annual meeting was held in Washington, D.C., in May 1950. The members received VIP treatment at the Library of Congress; indeed, both Luther Evans, the Librarian of Congress, and Wayne Grover, the Archivist of the United States, attended most sessions. A panel on forgeries and mistaken identities was well attended, and a panel on Civil

War material was moderated by Paul M. Angle, a Lincoln biographer. Amid much bonhomie, Dick Lederer succeeded Fields as Society president.

Thanks to Otto Eisenschiml, the Chicago chemist who had been threatened with having his gallbladder reimplanted by Dr. Thorek, the Washington meeting was more than a series of exhibits and panels. Eisenschiml was dean of the country's conspiracy theorists; his 1937 book *Why Was Lincoln Murdered?* was "a fascinating romp through a maze of circumstantial evidence leading nowhere but implying the complicity of Stanton."[13] A charter member of the NSAC, Eisenschiml seized upon the Washington meeting as an opportunity not only to restage the assassination but to do so at Ford's Theatre, which at that time was owned by the government but had not yet been restored. Nat Stein informed the New York chapter that Eisenschiml had arranged for the reconstruction of the stage and presidential box in time for the NSAC meeting. In the restaging, Eisenschiml would take the part of John Wilkes Booth; the other characters would be played by members of the Drama Department of George Washington University, under the direction of Professor Edwin P. Mangrum.[14]

Not everyone was enthusiastic about this portion of the Washington program. Alex Armour wrote to Fields, "Southern friends express horror at the reviving, in such a dramatic manner . . . an event which might happily be forgotten."[15] But Eisenschiml proceeded with his plans. He even located and borrowed, from an institution in Baltimore, the actual costumes worn on that fateful night.

The only trouble was that no one had bothered to seek the necessary permission from the Department of the Interior. Word of the proposed restaging leaked out, and it was viewed in some quarters as being in questionable taste. A phone call from a White House functionary denied the use of Ford's Theatre to the Society and threatened to abort the performance altogether. Somewhat daringly, the Library of Congress came to the rescue. The reenactment could be staged at the Library's Coolidge Auditorium! The reenactment was duly reported in the Library's newsletter:

> The curtain still drawn, Dr. Eisenschiml walked up onto the stage, took a position at its center, and step by step reviewed the progress of the conspiracy from the moment when the United States had declined to exchange prisoners with the Confederacy until about ten o'clock in the evening of that Good Friday long ago. At that point, the curtains were drawn back and the audience watched a scene from Tom Taylor's *Our American Cousin*. As it progressed, Mr. and Mrs. Lincoln, accompanied by Major Rathbone and Miss Harris, entered the flag-draped box . . . an offstage band played "Hail to the Chief," and the presidential party happily acknowledged the plaudits of their countrymen. . . .

At the moment when only "Asa" (*Our American Cousin*) was alone on the stage, delivering a boisterous soliloquy, Booth stole into the box, shot the President in the head, struggled momentarily with Major Rathbone . . . jumped onto the stage, breaking his leg, and ran haltingly across the platform and disappeared into the far wings. In a second there came the sound of clattering hooves in the alley. It was played "straight," with meticulous attention to detail.[16]

The Society was able to build on the successful Washington meeting with one in New York City the next year, which drew even better reviews. Perhaps no annual meeting before or since has better combined the elements that make for an appealing convention: prominent speakers, instructive panels, a members' exhibit, and opportunities to buy and sell autographs.

The question of how "pricey" an annual meeting should be is one that has never been completely resolved. Headquarters for the Washington meeting had been the dowdy Dodge Hotel, a concession to those most eager to make the occasion affordable. The 1951 meeting was aimed more at the carriage trade, with the Barbizon Plaza the official hotel and the events divided between the hotel and the host New-York Historical Society.

For the entire three-day meeting, a dealer bourse operated in the east mezzanine of the hotel. The banquet speaker was Catherine Drinker Bowen, whose prizewinning biographies included *Yankee from Olympus* and *John Adams and the American Revolution*. One panel discussion considered various aspects of the teaching of history; another discussed the variant handwriting of John Adams, Benjamin Franklin, and others. Arthur Swann provided members with a special preview of material to be auctioned at the Parke-Bernet Galleries.

The main attraction, however, was the exhibit by members at the New-York Historical Society. In contrast to the Ann Arbor convention, which focused on Revolutionary themes, collectors at the New York meeting were encouraged to exhibit the most interesting items in their collections without regard to period. Frank Pleadwell's display of Washington Irving's draft *Knickerbocker History of New York* was one of the most popular exhibits. The wife of one participant, not otherwise identified, told a newspaper reporter at the exhibit that collectors' wives were not a flashy crowd. "You won't see any mink coats here," she said. "Our mink coats are hanging on our husbands' walls."[17]

CHAPTER 3

"History in Your Hand"

A Los Angeles book collector, fresh from a visit to New York City in 1956, reflected on changes in the world of rare books:

> The antiquarian bookshop, it seemed to me, is disappearing from New York City life. . . . The Fourth Avenue shops are not what they were twenty years ago, and are hardly worth a visit. More entertaining, but not a great deal more rewarding . . . is a tour of the Greenwich Village shops. These are scattered, and are usually very small operations, with meager stocks.[1]

The autograph world, too, was changing, but slowly. Perhaps half a dozen dealers put out regular lists or did a major portion of their trade in autographs. But a harbinger of what lay ahead was the stunning success of the Oliver R. Barrett sale at New York's Parke-Bernet Galleries in February 1952. There, Barrett's legendary collection of Lincolniana was knocked down for a total of $273,610 in frenetic bidding. A franking signature of Lincoln as postmaster of New Salem went for $1,600. A page from the young Lincoln's sum book brought $3,600. A copy of the Thirteenth Amendment, signed by Lincoln, Vice President Hamlin, and many members of Congress, went for $4,400. An article in the *Autograph Collectors' Journal* noted that although most of the more valuable lots went to institutions, especially the Illinois State Historical Library, the balance of the 842 lots was bought by more than 100 private collectors.[2]

Charles Hamilton, then a relatively new dealer, had mixed feelings about the Barrett sale; he thought that the dumping of such a volume of Lincoln material at one time would glut the market for years.[3] Hamilton was wrong. Glut or no, the publicity attending the sale fired a national interest in Lincoln that was never far from the surface and drew a new generation of collectors into autographs.

For decades, American collectors had been most attracted to the Revolutionary period. Autographs of the likes of Franklin and Washington were readily available, while rarities like Button Gwinnett and Thomas Lynch Jr. lent zest to any quest for a complete set of the Signers of the Declaration of Independence. Collecting interests, however, were changing, and perhaps for the better. David Mearns wrote privately to Colton Storm, disparaging the preoccupation with Signers:

For grown men—packs of 'em—to chase after Signers is just about the most puerile and fatuous exercise that ever was invented. Most of the "immortal fifty-six"— there may have been half a dozen exceptions—were incredibly dull fellows who cashed in on a glorious moment of mob hysteria.[4]

The Barrett sale preceded by two months the NSAC annual meeting, which in 1952 convened at Harvard University in Cambridge, Massachusetts. As in New York, the meeting included a dealer bourse and an exhibit by members. Although the latter was on a smaller scale than in New York City, autographs on view included a document signed by both of Columbus's sponsors, King Ferdinand and Queen Isabella of Spain, and an Aztec codex, executed on the bark of a fig tree in about A.D. 1500, depicting the explorer Hernando Cortez speaking to Indian chiefs near Mexico City.[5] Other highlights of the meeting included a talk by Reginald Allen on collecting Gilbert and Sullivan material and a panel discussion on literary manuscripts. There was a consensus among those at Cambridge that the journal should seek a better balance between historical and literary material, and the editor, George Crosbie, promised to commission more articles on literary subjects.

Elsewhere, the New York chapter succeeded in gaining the first notable television exposure for autograph collecting. A representative of New York City station WNBT, who had attended the autograph pavilion at the 1950 antiques show, approached Crosbie with a suggestion for a half-hour TV program on historic autographs. Crosbie was more than amenable, and by the time negotiations had been completed the agreement called for four programs, a half hour each on the Declaration of Independence, George Washington, the Civil War, and American music. Produced by Steve Krantz and hosted by Charles F. McCarthy, "History in Your Hand" featured material from the collections of Joseph Fields, Nat Stein, and Richard Maass, among others. In the words of one reviewer:

Educational [television] does a neat job in dishing up history palatably. Produced in cooperation with the National Society of Autograph Collectors . . . the program gets a new slant on study of the past by presenting history through its raw materials. . . .

On the preem [*sic*] Sunday the subject was Lincoln. Emcee Charles F. McCarthy had as guests three authorities on Lincolniana, Charles Eberstadt, Jules Sindic and Nathaniel E. Stein. Background was set with a short biography of the Emancipator, narrated by McCarthy against a set of excellent drawings of scenes from Lincoln's life.

The trio of experts then exhibited items from their collections: a check for $5 the President made out to "Lucy (colored woman)"; a playbill for Ford's Theatre for the fateful evening when Lincoln was shot; the telegram to Gen. Grant informing him of the assassination.[6]

It is a commentary on contemporary television that a proposal for a program such as "History in Your Hand" would today be laughed out of virtually any TV studio. In 1952, however, responsible producers still viewed television as an educational as well as an entertainment medium. "History in Your Hand" aired on four August Sundays. Although the programs ran in a "slow" ratings month, WNBT received more than 500 requests for a facsimile Washington letter that the station offered to anyone who called in.[7]

In a press interview at the time of the 1950 Washington, D.C., meeting, Joe Fields told a local reporter, "For heaven's sake, emphasize that we are not a bunch of bobby-soxers running around collecting crooners' autographs."[8]

This distinction between celebrity-chasers and "serious" collectors was on the minds of many of the collectors who represented the core of the 600-member NSAC. At the Cambridge meeting, the most controversial motion was one that proposed that the Society change its name to The Manuscript Society, with a view to distinguishing its members from the bobby-soxers. Secretary-Treasurer Maass noted in his minutes that the proposed change was the subject of "considerable spirited discussion."[9] The new president, Justin Turner, appointed a committee composed of Gordon Banks, Watt Marchman, Colton Storm, and David Mearns to consider the propriety of a name change. All of them favored the idea.

The rank and file of the Society did not appear to feel strongly about the name change, but there was considerable correspondence among the directors. David Mearns wrote to Banks:

Can we agree on "The Manuscript Society?" To my mind the advantages are obvious. It does away with the tawdry immaturity and vulgar connotation of *autograph* and replaces it with a more appropriate and therefore a more dignified word. By dropping the restrictive *Collectors* from the title, a larger membership of scholars becomes eligible.[10]

The committee published its report in the Summer 1952 issue of the journal, recommending that the NSAC adopt a new name—The Manuscript Society—and call its journal *Manuscripts*. When the journal opened its pages to persons of divergent views, a vigorous exchange developed. Two committee members, Gordon Banks and Colton Storm, presented the case in favor:

Banks: "I am heartily in favor of the new name. . . . I am convinced that it is not
      quantity of members that we need but quality."

Storm: "The use of the word *autograph* has troubled me for as long as the Society
      has been in existence. The word *collectors* had not disturbed me particularly,
      but I understand . . . that the word is restrictive."[11]

Among those leading the "nays" were Dick Lederer and one Norma Cuthbert:

Lederer: "We can't afford to lose the million [*sic*] we've already invested in the
      autograph name. How many letters of explanation would be needed to solicit
      under any other name and how many [collectors] would refuse to join because
      they don't collect manuscripts?"

Cuthbert: "I prefer the name as it is. It certainly is true that many people, especially
      in the environs of Hollywood, think of an autograph as a signature only. And
      the word perhaps does reek of bobby-soxers, but that is just why a society
      should strive to restore to the term the dignity it deserves."[12]

The most eloquent dissent came from the Society's secretary, Walter Eastburn, who wrote to President Turner:

I disagree with the committee report; first, because the committee seems to have been packed with a preponderance of "manuscriptophiles and bibliophiles" rather than an equal number of such creatures and "autograph collectors and dealers." . . .

I disagree . . . secondly, because I think [we are losing sight of] the fact that practically every collector of today started out by acquiring some person's signature. . . .

Thirdly, I disagree with the committee report because of my fear that eventually the collectors of large volume stuff (books and manuscripts) may swallow up the small volume collectors of signatures, letters and documents if the Society name drops "autograph."[13]

A few members sought a compromise. Turner ruminated about a name such as The Manuscript Collectors' Society, and London dealer Winifred Myers suggested The National Society of Autograph and Manuscript Collectors. Eastburn and Maass floated The Autograph and Manuscript Society.

When the issue came to a vote at the directors' meeting that preceded the annual business meeting in 1953, the directors scheduled a straight vote on whether or not to change the name to The Manuscript Society as recommended. After perfunctory debate, the board approved the change by a vote of 12 to 2, with one abstention. Although the board had the authority to make the change on its own, it decided to seek a ratifying vote by the general membership the following day. The board's action was duly approved at the business meeting.

The change of name was of more than cosmetic significance. With a single vote, the Society had taken the words *autograph* and *collector* out of its title. It had broadened its base and had by implication become more inclusive, but it had also planted the seeds of an identity crisis.

Formalities at the 1953 meeting at Columbus, Ohio, were dominated by the Society's name change and expressions of regret at the passing of charter member Dick Lederer. The three-day program, however, was an imaginative one. The Ohio State Museum had prepared a special autograph exhibit. Panel subjects included "Manuscripts and the Historian" and autographs in the undercollected fields of business and labor Americana.

The greatest interest centered on the panel "What Shall I Do with My Collection?" The opening paper was to be delivered by Joseph Fields, but he had been recalled by the Navy for the Korean War, and his paper was read by the incoming president, Colton Storm. According to Fields, the main ways of disposing of a collection are by gift during the collector's lifetime, by bequest, by sale as a collection, and by sale by lot to a dealer or through an auction house. The panel included representatives of the Yale University Library, the University of Pennsylvania, Parke-Bernet Galleries, and the dealer community, and so each disposal mode found supporters.[14]

At the time of the Society's meeting in 1953, membership hovered around 670, with some three-quarters of members from the East Coast and the Greater Chicago area. Cash in the bank, including $1,200 from the Columbus auction, was around $6,000. The Society's main expense continued to be its journal, for which printing costs were running slightly more than $1,000 per issue. But the Society's finances were sufficiently stable that it now had a "paid employee." The journal editor, George Crosbie Jr., was voted a salary of $200 per issue.[15]

**Prime Minister Churchill to Senior Military Officials
19 July 1940**

Let it be very clearly understood that all directions emanating from me are to be made in writing, or should be immediately afterwards confirmed in writing, and that I do not accept any responsibility for matters relating to national defense on which I am alleged to have given decisions unless they are recorded in writing.

—Winston S. Churchill, *Their Finest Hour*

The Manuscript Society sought the best of both worlds. It prided itself on being a national organization, but it hoped to stimulate local chapters so that collectors could meet and socialize with their fellows between annual meetings. Such chapters were active in New York and Los Angeles, and in 1951 Boston joined the ranks. On November 8, with Gordon Banks as host, 27 New England collectors met at the Club of Odd Volumes to set up a local group. Richard Maass spoke briefly of the activities of the New York group, including the TV series. More than most regional groups, the New England chapter moved its meetings from one locale to another. In the fall of 1953, for instance, the New Englanders met at the Rhode Island Historical Society in Providence.[16]

The Los Angeles chapter met four times during 1951–52. One session heard Frank Pleadwell of Honolulu, a charter member, on the subject of James Boswell's travels. Seventy-five persons attended a joint meeting with the Southern California Broadcasters Association for a music exhibit. Two other joint meetings were held, one with the Antiquarian Booksellers Association of America, another with the Lincoln Fellowship of Southern California.[17]

The New York chapter, however, continued to set the pace. In September 1952, members attended a preview of a Lincoln documentary slated for television. In December the chapter met at the home of Otto von Kienbusch, who displayed his fine collection of armor. Three months later the host was Carl Tollefsen, who exhibited his collection of musical instruments and autographs of the great composers.[18]

The 1954 annual meeting, at New Haven, Connecticut, was the Society's first under its new name. It continued the tried and true combination of formal presentations, panel discussions, and autograph auctions that had become the principal source of revenue for the Society's journal, now called *Manuscripts*.

The panel discussion was on the economics of autograph collecting. Richard Maass focused on the rising demand; Gordon Banks discussed the implications of dwindling supply. A second panel considered means of displaying autograph material. The banquet speaker, Civil War historian David M. Potter, spoke on "The Collector and the Historian." Meanwhile, Yale University put on a special exhibit of its finest manuscripts, from a Babylonian cylinder dating from 2500 B.C. to selections from the papers of Henry L. Stimson.

At the business meeting, Maass succeeded Colton Storm as president. Storm had served only one year when he had to step down because of ill health. Walter Eastburn—a retired railroad executive whose collecting interests ranged from presidential franks to signers of the Israeli declaration of independence—became secretary-treasurer.

A record 170 Manuscript Society members and guests attended the elaborate 1955 meeting, held at three Virginia locales over three and a half days. Registration was on Thursday, May 26, in Richmond, where the first order of business was a visit to the Liggett & Myers cigarette factory. Friday was devoted to an extended visit to Monticello, where members heard a talk on Jeffersonian architecture and attended the business meeting. On Saturday, members were guests of the Virginia Historical Society in Richmond; the banquet speaker was the Pulitzer Prize–winning Civil War historian Bruce Catton, and the auction that followed his address netted the Society a record $1,368. On Sunday, May 29, members toured Williamsburg by way of historic Shirley Plantation.

The Manuscript Society, in six years, had achieved many of the original objectives of its founders. It had established a national organization and put it on a reasonably sound financial footing. Its annual meetings provided a forum for collectors and others to meet and to socialize. The journal, though struggling, showed promise. Yet to some extent the Society was becoming a victim of its own success. Having provided collectors, dealers, and institutional members with an organization, it was reduced at times to discussing the size and format of membership certificates.

All this was about to change. At the board of directors' meeting in Richmond, Robert Metzdorf of the Yale University Library outlined the history of the papers relating to the Lewis and Clark expedition, which were subject to replevin by the United States after having been in private hands for more than 150 years. The threat to institutions and private collectors alike was clear. There was work to be done, and the Manuscript Society would play an important role.

CHAPTER 4

David and Goliath: The Lewis and Clark Case

Over the years, the tendency of government organizations to purge old files has given autograph collectors some remarkable opportunities. Around 1919, for instance, the State Department needed additional room in what is now the Executive Office Building on Pennsylvania Avenue. Quantities of dead files, including thousands of documents signed by nineteenth-century presidents, were carted into a courtyard and burned. The sight of so many presidential signatures appears to have stimulated the curiosity of the clerks, who rescued some of the documents as souvenirs.

The federal government's initial indifference to old records came to the fore in a different context several decades later. In 1952, descendants of a Union officer in the Civil War, General John Henry Hammond, donated to the Minnesota Historical Society an old desk that had belonged to the general. Shortly thereafter, members of the historical society staff opened a drawer of the desk and discovered, wrapped in newspaper, a treasure trove of manuscripts. These included, in addition to some of Hammond's own papers, unpublished field notes of the Lewis and Clark expedition of 1803–1806.

Even before the ink was dry on the Louisiana Purchase, President Jefferson had obtained from Congress an appropriation for exploration of the vast new territory. Early in 1803, he ordered his personal secretary, Captain Meriwether Lewis, and Lieutenant William Clark, both Army officers, to conduct an overland exploration. Their odyssey, which took them up the Missouri River, across the Dakotas, and through the Rockies to the Pacific, was remarkable not only for its scope but for the loss of only one life among a party of explorers who spent more than two years in the wilderness.

The Hammond family papers, most in the hand of William Clark, were a major historical find. Whereas the published journals of the expedition dated from January 1804, Clark's notes began in December 1803, some seven weeks earlier. The newly discovered notes—67 pages in all—included descriptions of the countryside, interviews with Indians, and comments on the health of expedition members on the march from St. Louis, Missouri, to Bismarck, North Dakota. There were drawings of a keel boat, Indian burial mounds, and maps, some in ink and others in watercolor.[1] No one knew how the papers had come into the possession of the Hammond family. Later, however, it appeared that General Hammond had in the 1870s headed an Indian agency at Lawrence, Kansas, on an Army post once occupied by William Clark.

Press reports of the find reached the Hammond heirs, who were appalled at what they had let slip through their fingers. They maintained that they had donated a desk to the historical society, not papers with a value estimated in the press at between $15,000 and $50,000. To settle the question of title, the Hammond trustees sued the Minnesota Historical Society for return of the documents.

In 1954 the federal government entered the picture. The Justice Department, acting for the National Archives, entered a claim for the Clark papers on behalf of the U.S. government. Assistant Solicitor General J. Lee Rankin asserted that because Captain Clark had been a government employee, his notes while on official business were government property. Equally important, he asserted that, even though they had been effectively discarded many years before, the papers remained government property. In a pretrial deposition the Justice Department contended that individuals and museums were rarely in a position to give records proper care, and that when papers remained in the hands of individuals and private institutions they were largely inaccessible to the public. Robert Bahmer, the assistant archivist of the United States, issued a statement on October 11, 1955, elaborating on these points:

When Federal records which we believe were not lawfully alienated from Federal custody are found under conditions inimical to their continued preservation and use as public records, we would be remiss in our responsibilities as Federal employees and professional archivists if we counselled inaction.

Not content with asserting ownership of the Clark papers, Bahmer went on to suggest that documents of such importance should not be in private hands:

We do not believe that historical scholarship would be served by permitting the Clark papers to remain in private hands. These documents belong to the Nation.[2]

The threat of replevin was not a new one. As early as 1943, Michigan dealer Forest Sweet had raised the subject in an address before the Society of American Archivists:

One of the officers of your Society [tells] of a smallish man who took a colonial record book to the head of a state archives, asking "What will you give me for that?" A moment's glance was enough to discover that the item had once been part of the public records. The archivist reached for a rubber stamp, inked it, and applied it to the record book: "Property of the State of _____ ," at the same time answering, "Not one cent."

Sweet went on to consider the implications of his anecdote:

But is that really the end of the story? What did the state gain? The state gained the fugitive record book. What did the state lose? Did the little man have a trunkful of similar records or a garage full? If he did, what became of them? If he didn't have them, did the little man know where there were other colonial records from which he may have bought or borrowed this single item to test the market? If he stole it, why wasn't he questioned and then prosecuted for the theft? . . . Perhaps we shall never know just what the state lost but we can count one loss quite certainly: The little man brought in nothing else.[3]

The 1954 suit with respect to the Clark papers marked the first instance in which the U.S. government had sued to reclaim historical manuscripts in the possession of private individuals. Robert Metzdorf, curator of manuscripts at Yale, wrote to Richard Maass that endorsement of the government's position "would be a death-blow to private collecting in a wide section of Americana."[4]

Although institutions had as great a stake in the outcome as private collectors, the challenge to the government position was led by the Manuscript Society, and within it by President Richard Maass and the former president, Justin Turner. At its annual meeting in Richmond, the Society created a Manuscripts Emergency Committee, headed by Turner, to raise money and to intervene as amicus curiae in the Hammond family suit. The Society's action gained national attention. The *New York Times* wrote:

The resolution approved [by the Manuscript Society] asserted that if the Government's position was maintained perhaps as much as 40 percent of the holdings of historical societies and public and private libraries would be subject to Government confiscation. . . .

Mr. Maass said the society maintained that the Government "has abandoned thousands of documents" in 175 years by not putting them into archives. That, he declared, establishes the private collector's rights to them.[5]

Although the federal government, with its seemingly limitless resources, was not an entity to be challenged lightly, the Manuscript Society found numerous institutional allies, including Metzdorf of the Yale University Library, Watt Marchman of the Hayes Memorial Library, Gordon Williams of the UCLA Library, and Paul Angle, now director of the Chicago Historical Society. Institutional support for the Society was not unanimous, however. Lyman Butterfield, editor in chief of the John Adams Papers and a onetime Manuscript Society director, wrote to Maass that he was "very much upset" by the Society's position relative to the Clark papers, a position that he called "hasty and more than likely mistaken."[6]

An article in *Manuscripts* set forth the Society's position:

It seems clear that this action on the part of the government is an attempt to establish in the National Archives title to all official papers of all government employees, no matter when made or under what conditions. If sustained, the court action might establish a precedent whereby the Archivist of the United States could claim possession of any such document, whether in a public library, state collection, university library, historical society or private collection. . . .

The present claim of the Federal government disregards the mode of acquisition of any such material—whether by gift, bequest, purchase, or discovery—and the well-known "vacuum cleaner" technique will evidently be applied. It seems improper for the government to claim to be the sole agency capable of properly caring for material of national historical interest. Little or no interest in our national historical manuscripts was shown by any government agency except the Library of Congress until 1934, when the Federal government finally established the National Archives.[7]

The Manuscript Society archives contain more correspondence on the Clark case than on any other single subject. A letter from Turner to Robert Metzdorf conveys some of the urgency of the moment:

I started the ball rolling yesterday and have an appointment with a representative of the Associated Press tomorrow. . . .

[I believe] there is a new president of the American Booksellers Association. You had better check on it and if I am correct contact the new President. . . . I think it would be a good idea to also contact the individual chapters and attempt to obtain a resolution from each of them.[8]

The Society distributed 3,000 copies of an article from its journal, "A Government Threat to Manuscript Collections." Eventually, some $1,800 would be collected and contributed to the Hammond defense.[9]

The case went to trial in the U.S. District Court, St. Paul, on December 13, 1955, and continued for four days. Government witnesses maintained that Clark's rough notes for the first part of the expedition were as "official" as the later final report. Several speculated that Clark's notes had been unlawfully removed from government files by General Hammond. Witnesses for the Hammond family sought to prove that Clark's notes were essentially personal and that they had always been in private hands. The Justice Department's position that only the government could take care of such historic papers was undermined by evidence that all of the official reports from the Lewis and Clark expedition that had been sent to Washington had been lost! This fact provided an opening for the Hammond family and the Manuscript Society's counsel, Dermot Stanley of the New York firm of McKenzie, Hyde, Willson, French, and Poor. The defense, using research done by Donald Hyde, demonstrated that the government's treatment of historical materials before the establishment of the National Archives had been a sorry tale of neglect and indifference.

Gunnar H. Nordbye, chief justice of the District Court of Minnesota, delivered his decision on December 17, 1955.

The Government's position is that Lewis, as leader of the Expedition, was under strict injunction by President Jefferson to prepare notes; . . . that the President expressly ordered Lewis to make a written record of his observations by means of a "journal, notes and observations of every kind." Therefore, it is argued that Clark, who was a co-commander with Lewis, was likewise within the ambit of Jefferson's instructions and that these rough notes became, and continued to be, the property of the Government. . . . It is pointed out that the Government went to great expense, considerably more than the $2,500 appropriated by Congress, in financing the Expedition, and that, generally speaking, the work product of government officers should belong to the Government. . . . In addition, the Government urges that there is circumstantial evidence that [Clark's] rough notes came into Hammond's possession when he liquidated the Central Superintendency of Indian Affairs at Lawrence, Kansas, in 1878.

But Judge Nordbye went on to note that the government had not treated other reports on the Lewis and Clark expedition as government property. Indeed, three of Clark's later journals had been turned over to the American Philosophical Society in Philadelphia, with the approval of both Jefferson and Clark. This fact placed a very heavy burden on the government in its contention that Clark's notes were government records. Judge Nordbye noted that although Clark's notes might be of great interest to twentieth-century scholars, "the Government was not concerned with such aspects of the papers in 1806. Certainly every inference to be deduced from the evidence herein supports the contention that Captain Clark considered these notes as his personal property." Nordbye continued:

The Hammond heirs were in possession of these notes in 1953, and every indication is that General Hammond and his family had been in such possession for many, many years. . . . The Government cannot contend successfully that it has any title to the notes in controversy merely because at some time they may have been left by Clark in some depository or desk available to him when he was the Indian agent. . . . These notes had no relation to the affairs of the Agency. . . . The position of the Government in claiming title to these papers in controversy upon the assumption that General Hammond wrongly abstracted them from the Lawrence, Kansas, office in 1878 is too tenuous and speculative to provide a basis for a factual finding of title in the Government.[10]

Expressions of relief at the verdict from collectors and museums were short-lived, for the government indicated its intention to appeal. Nearly two years elapsed before the appeal was heard in St. Louis on November 19, 1957. There, the government's attorney, George C. Doub, contended that the fact that the Clark papers were rough notes did not preclude their being government property. The government had a right to all such papers, he said, making the sweeping assertion, "It is time that it be established that every document prepared by a Government official should be the property of the Government."[11]

On January 23, 1958, the three judges of the court of appeals unanimously upheld the lower court's decision in favor of the Hammond family, reiterating that the Clark papers were personal in nature and had been preserved in private hands. The court implicitly rejected the government's claim that every document prepared by a government official was federal property—a contention that, had it been upheld, would have been even more threatening to private collectors than a narrowly based decision in favor of the government in the matter of the Clark papers. With this decision the government dropped its case, and the Minnesota Historical Society withdrew its claim as well.

The Hammond family was grateful to the Manuscript Society and its allies. Louis Starr, on behalf of the family, wrote to members of the Emergency Committee of his pleasure "in the successful pursuit of a principle in the face of many obstacles. . . . We are not collectors, but the Government was attempting to take from us papers that had been in our possession for more than 75 years—and without any compensation whatever."[12]

Quite apart from the impact on the Hammond family, the government's unsuccessful replevin threatened to make manuscripts less accessible to the public, rather than, as Rankin had contended, more accessible. Had the government been successful, few collectors or institutions would have felt safe in acknowledging ownership of historic documents, much less in putting them on display. Richard Maass, writing in *Manuscripts*, took satisfaction in the outcome, but expressed disappointment in the reactions of some institutions that he had contacted:

Wholehearted support, financial and otherwise, was received from a number of individual members and institutions. However, it was shocking to find that some institutions with the greatest stake in the outcome of the case . . . were reluctant to participate in the trial. Two libraries found legal excuses, two others were afraid of "unfavorable publicity."[13]

Robert Metzdorf wrote to Walter Eastburn, "The Manuscript Society has come out of this with colors flying. . . . Those who doubted and held back should realize that they missed a chance to stand up and be counted."[14] The Society's attorney, Donald Hyde, thought that the fact that the National Archives had been stopped at the district court level was "of the greatest importance" to collectors.[15] Justin Turner, too, thought that the fact that the government had lost a test in which it had set forth a fairly strong case would have "a salutary effect."[16] But over the long term, the hopes of private collectors that the threat of replevin would recede were not to be realized.

CHAPTER 5

Growing Pains

In 1956 the Society held its annual meeting in Chicago. Perhaps because the Society traced its origins to the Windy City, four institutions—the Northwestern University Library, the Chicago Historical Society, the University of Chicago Library, and the Newberry Library—mounted special exhibitions to mark the occasion.

On the first day of the meeting, members went to the Evanston campus of Northwestern University, where they heard a panel discussion on manuscript preservation at the Deering Library. The library exhibit featured a section on American literature, including authors Walt Whitman, Ezra Pound, Gertrude Stein, Carl Sandburg, and H. L. Mencken. A letter of Mencken describing his ingredients for a successful short story, seemed as applicable in 1956 and today as when it was written: "Characters of today, intelligent, sophisticated, well-to-do; the story of a sex conflict, satirically treated. The more action, of course, the better."[1]

Over the next two days, visits to the other participating institutions were interspersed with the Society's business meeting and auction. The Chicago gathering featured the first members' exhibit in four years. Nat Stein, a stockbroker with a special interest in presidential autographs, was elected president to succeed Richard Maass. There was considerable discussion of a recent decision by the British government that no manuscript valued at more than £100 could leave the country until it was photographed and a copy deposited in the British Museum. Collectors complained that this requirement would permit researchers in Britain to use copies of American-owned originals without authorization from the actual owner. In its business meeting the Society passed a resolution associating itself with other groups that were protesting Britain's action. In response to these and other protests, the British eventually modified the regulation in question.

Since the Society's inception, its directors had held a meeting at least once in the fall or winter, in addition to the board meeting during the annual convention. Because there were fewer distractions, these fall meetings were often more productive than those in May. The board meeting on October 5, 1956, was held at President Stein's Manhattan apartment and ran over to a second day. In general, members expressed satisfaction with recent annual meetings. Attendees had enjoyed the programs, and the auctions—proceeds of which were divided evenly between the consigner and the Society—had generated essential revenue.

The Society's two main problems concerned membership—it was now losing two members for every three new recruits—and editorial problems with *Manuscripts*. The journal was a particular source of concern. According to the treasurer, the cost of printing the journal absorbed $4.37 of each member's $5.00 annual dues. There were problems, too, of substance and editing. After an initial flurry of fine articles, some of which were definitive discussions of the autographs of persons such as Button Gwinnett, John Adams, and John Dickinson, a succession of editors had found it difficult to obtain articles of sufficiently broad appeal. As early as 1951 and 1952 the journal was including articles like "Library of Congress Notes" and institutional handouts such as "Literary and Historical Manuscripts in the Clark Memorial Library." No ready solution was apparent. Several years later, director David Coblentz wrote to Herbert Klingelhofer: "I am still of the opinion that we need to popularize our journal a bit more. I would hate to see it become nothing more than an arena where one library or institution parades all its latest acquisitions."[2]

In 1955, advertisers could have a full-page ad for $80 or a quarter-page ad for $25. A full-page ad on the back cover of the journal carried a certain cachet, however, and put the Society in the middle of a squabble between two dealers. A 1954 memo from President Richard Maass to members of the Publications Committee suggests the kind of bickering with which they had to deal:

Since the annual meeting a complaint on advertising policy in *Manuscripts* has arisen. Specifically, the complaint is as follows: Dealer A, a long-time member of The Manuscript Society, as well as an advertiser, has complained because Dealer B was allotted a favored location for his ad [on the back cover] while . . . Dealer A had space inside the magazine. Dealer B has not been a constant advertiser and at one time resigned from The Manuscript Society. . . . Dealer A feels he has been unjustly discriminated against in spite of his loyalty and support to the organization.

Dealer A has been contacted and I hope placated. On page 128 of the current issue of *Manuscripts* is a small paragraph explaining the placement of advertisements in the magazine. Apparently, Dealer A did not notice that the advertising spaces were to be rotated in position and that before long he, too, would become eligible for "that favored spot."[3]

The Society was paying Crosbie the grand sum of $200 per issue, but its finances did not permit the hiring of a full-time professional. In 1954 the directors decided to offer a $50 honorarium for the most interesting article in each issue and a $100 prize for the best article in a calendar year. Tinkering continued. On the theory that the existing size of the 64-page magazine, $9^1/_2$ by $6^1/_2$ inches, was inconvenient, the board switched in 1955 to a more compact $8^1/_2$-by-$5^1/_2$-inch format. Whatever the size, quality control continued to be a problem.

In 1955 Crosbie gave up the editorship; he was succeeded first by Howard Tribolet and then by Norman Dodge. Dodge resigned because of ill health after one year; he was followed by Nat Stein's son-in-law, Jack Zeldes, a lawyer-collector from Connecticut. Zeldes did not care for the new, smaller journal format; he told the board in November 1957 that a return to the larger size would permit greater variety in headings, illustrations, and insertions. At the November 1957 board meeting, however, Justin Turner opposed any change in format, observing that too frequent changes were "not beneficial."[4] Joseph Fields wrote that a change would annoy members and institutions who routinely bound back issues. Meanwhile, Zeldes's position was weakened when the Fall 1957 issue, his first as editor, appeared with one of two cover illustrations printed upside down. His proposal was rebuffed.[5]

An immediate result of that board meeting was that a director, Clyde Walton of Iowa, was appointed to head an ad hoc committee to see whether *Manuscripts* could associate itself with some university press. Walton proposed to several institutions that the Society would continue to finance the production costs of its journal if the host press would provide an editor.[6] Despite hints of "a substantial gift program" from rich autograph collectors, there were no takers. In December 1957 President Stein announced an increase in dues, with regular membership raised from $5.00 to $7.50. The increase was necessitated, he said, by rising costs involved in producing the journal.

In 1958, a member of the board sent the Society's president a memorandum in which he discussed a number of issues, but especially *Manuscripts*. "It is obvious that we are scraping the barrel for articles," he wrote.

The lack of a large number of articles that might serve as a backlog, from which we can afford to be selective, still continues to plague us. The editorship, next to the presidency the most important office in the organization, continues to be a veritable parade passing in review. That each [editor] should have his own ideas and opinions is only natural and human. I think an effort should be made to obtain an editor for a period of longer than a year or two. Editors that can fill our requirements are difficult to come by.[7]

The Society's tenth annual meeting was held at a dramatic location, the newly opened Motel on the Mountain, overlooking the Hudson Valley at Suffern, New York. The meeting included an extensive discussion of recent developments in the Lewis and Clark case and a tour of nearby West Point.

Behind the bonhomie was an undercurrent of dissatisfaction among some of the founding directors. Forest Sweet professed to be "weary" of the Society, complaining that it had lost all initiative because of the hostility of certain dealers toward it.[8] Justin Turner deplored the fact that the Society was attracting too few collectors to the annual meetings—he doubted that half of those attending could be truly characterized as collectors.[9]

The Society continued to deal with its problems through a 15-person board that was probably too large. The real work was done by a hardcore group that included Justin Turner, David Mearns, Nat Stein, Howard Tribolet, Richard Maass, and Herbert Klingelhofer. One board member's memorandum to a colleague minced no words:

As always, the Board of Directors has been loaded with people who do not produce—drones so to speak. I have argued for years that we should elect only those who we are certain will work. . . . I despair that we shall ever find fifteen *working* directors. The result has been that the president, in the past, has been hamstrung in his decisions.[10]

Many of the complaints about the Society had some basis in fact, but in broader terms the Society was achieving its objectives. Formed to improve communication among collectors, it had achieved this goal admirably. Even members who did not bother to attend annual meetings had access to other collectors through the Society's membership list. But having achieved this priority goal, the Society lacked a clear agenda beyond responding to threats to the private ownership of manuscripts.[11]

In accepting a large number of institutional members, the Society had diluted the role of the private collector. But this action had compensations, for it made the Society far more inclusive. As years went on, the role of planning and staffing annual meetings would move from individual directors to institutional members whose libraries and museums were familiar with the logistics of conference sponsorship.

Meanwhile, most people who attended the annual meetings enjoyed the camaraderie and the exchange of views. Few could resist an opportunity to recall their first introduction to autographs. At Suffern, historian George F. Scheer told Society members:

As a schoolboy I read in my father's library just the kind of books on American history you would expect to find on the shelves of an average American business-man with a taste for history. . . . One Sunday I discovered he had manuscripts, and I found myself reading actual letters from Jefferson, Washington, Tyler, Clay, and others; these quite ordinary letters suddenly revealed to me my kinship with the past, with these and other men long dead. I still remember a letter from Jefferson to a friend. Jefferson was hard up. He needed to sell some of his Poplar Forest lands to pay his debts. Well, we had been faced with the same thing.[12]

At the Suffern meeting, directors heard a strong plea from past president Justin Turner that the next convention be held in Los Angeles; the Califor-nian reminded his hearers that the Society, in its first 10 years, had never held an annual meeting west of the Mississippi. It now had many members in the Los Angeles area, and they were eager to act as hosts. He cited the Huntington Library and the University of Southern California as probable institutional hosts. Meeting at a time when the Society needed to plan its annual meetings only one year in advance, the directors accepted Turner's offer.

Of the 100 persons who attended the Los Angeles meeting in 1958, approximately half were from the East Coast. When President Stein deliv-ered a brief valedictory to the board, he took satisfaction in some improve-ments in *Manuscripts,* which in 1958 had been run jointly by members of the Publications Committee, but noted that his successor would have the responsibility of recruiting a permanent editor. He characterized the Society as in a healthy condition, but with a continuing need for new members and more solid finances.

Stein's successor as president was Gordon Banks, head of the autograph department at Goodspeed's Book Shop in Boston and, with Forest Sweet, one of a very few dealers who had supported the Society since its inception. Considering that the National Society of Autograph Collectors had for a brief period excluded dealers from its board, the choice of the tall, urbane Banks as Manuscript Society president was something of a milestone. An exchange of letters among several of the directors before the annual meeting had revealed strong support for Banks and no concern whatever about making a dealer president.

Richard Maass summarized the meeting in a letter to Walter Eastburn:

The next issue of *Manuscripts* will be handled by Banks and [Norman] Dodge in Boston until we have located a new editor. . . . It was decided that [Justin] Turner would head up a committee to obtain 25 patrons who would pledge $100 each to the Society for a period of two years. . . . It was unanimous that we not reduce the size or quality [of *Manuscripts*].

The meeting itself was magnificent, with all plans carefully made by Justin, and the institutions we visited were exciting. The weather was hot but pleasant and the hotel the best we have stayed in.[13]

One of the problems that any organization faces is the policing of its members. To what extent was the Manuscript Society responsible for the behavior—commercial and otherwise—of those who joined?

Officially, the Society took no responsibility for its members, with some interesting exceptions. In 1948 the application of a New York–area dealer with a record of pro-Nazi activities was rejected, apparently without explanation. Several years later, the application of a collector with a similar background was accepted, but Society directors breathed a collective sigh of relief when he showed no interest in attending annual meetings.

In 1952 President Maass was informed by several dealers that a member of the Society was not paying for his purchases. The member was not sent a renewal application, and in March 1953 Maass informed dealers by means of a circular that the person in question was no longer a member of the Society.[14] This constituted firm action by Society standards, but it is not clear what the directors would have done if the culprit had renewed his application. Some dealers appeared to hold the Society responsible for the credit rating of its members. In 1961 Mary Benjamin wrote a two-page letter to David Mearns detailing her problems with one Society member. "On numerous occasions in the past I have had distressing experiences," she wrote. "It is such experiences that discourage me from attending any [Manuscript Society] meetings."[15]

Considering the Society's reluctance to police its members, the fact that prospective members required a sponsor was something of an anomaly. The subject received a full airing at the directors' meeting at Philadelphia on January 30, 1959. There, the board agreed that the application procedure was cumbersome and that the requirement for a sponsor was a possible deterrent to applicants. Although Secretary Eastburn thought that applicants should be subject to more review rather than less, most other directors disagreed. A motion to abolish the requirement for a sponsor passed with only one dissenting vote.[16]

CHAPTER 6

Expanding Horizons

In its second decade, the Manuscript Society at times seemed preoccupied with problems of administration and finance. Nevertheless, it was contributing in an unobtrusive way to the public's knowledge of manuscripts and of the importance of historical preservation. During the Society's early years, most American cities had at least two newspapers, and virtually every annual meeting generated some press coverage. In their remarks to reporters, officers of the Society invariably stressed the importance of preserving America's written heritage.

The need for such education was great, as the state of New York inadvertently proved. Between 1951 and 1954, state offices disposed of a variety of old files, many of which were of no interest to anyone. Those slated for destruction, however, were housed in the same Albany warehouse as papers that had been designated as having special historical interest. A waste disposal firm made several pickups at the warehouse and, in the words of one archivist, the historic records "moved closer and closer to the elevator shaft." Eventually, in October 1954, they disappeared altogether.

After several months, the Onondaga County Historical Association alerted the state archivist to the fact that some documents that appeared to belong to the state had been found by a truck driver and turned over to the association. The association's president, Richard Wright, traced the papers to the Rolland Paper Company in Quebec, and was told that the company was indeed processing wastepaper from Albany and was about to turn its most recent shipment into pulp!

Wright asked the company to delay any further processing of material from Albany, and the company complied. Wright then contacted the state Division of Archives, which arranged for the return of the last shipment.

Despite the cooperation of the Rolland Paper Company, however, an estimated two-thirds of the documents once designated for preservation appear to have been destroyed.[1]

The Manuscript Society, meanwhile, marked the end of its first decade with a modest promotional pamphlet:

> More than a decade ago a small group of men and women were confident that the time was ripe for the banding together of those interested in the collecting and custody of manuscripts, letters, documents and related material. The only exclusive feature of this association was to be the common interest in original autographs in their various forms. We agreed that once the virus of seeking out this most intimate memento of the great, the near great, or some facet of history has got into your veins, you are a convert for life. . . .
>
> There are thousands of collectors throughout the world. We will never catch every one, but today we do have over 700 members in 11 countries, representing leading private collectors, dealers, librarians, historical societies, colleges and universities, in addition to numerous writers and researchers who have found membership helpful to their work.[2]

Notwithstanding this optimistic message, the Society was finding it difficult to expand its membership. Part of the problem lay with the local chapters. Those that were active, most notably the New York and Los Angeles groups, were led by a few established collectors. In part because local meetings were usually unpublicized, potential members rarely learned of them, and as a result the Society gained few grass-roots recruits.

The Washington, D.C., chapter was something of a case study. In 1959, at the request of Herbert Klingelhofer, Floyd Flickinger, and John Mayfield, the Society approved a chapter for the Greater Washington, D.C., area. During 1960 and 1961 the group met a number of times, with attendance running between 15 and 30 persons. The chapter promoted an exhibit of historical and literary autographs belonging to area members. The exhibit, for which the libraries provided appropriate mounts, appeared in several Washington, D.C., and suburban Maryland libraries and attracted some press notice.

In 1961, however, new officers were elected and the group fell on hard times. In 1963 the national board acknowledged its disappointment at the Society's performance at the local level and found the inactivity of the D.C. chapter especially vexing. The new Society president, the Reverend David Coblentz, was given blanket authority to appoint or dismiss chapter officers. The results were not dramatic, but the Washington, D.C., chapter, now led by Klingelhofer and Dorothy Eaton, enjoyed a modest resurgence. Ultimately, however, all regional groups would to some degree fall victim to television, urban congestion, and the disparate interests of individual members.

On a national level, the Society recognized the need for more and better publicity. Money was tight, however, and the means for improved publicity not readily discernible. In 1962 the board put an advertising executive, Milton Slater, in charge of public relations, but with an annual budget of only $500, his main achievement was to arrange for the exchange of ads with several related collector publications.

In the spring of 1961, Walter Eastburn—perhaps the only member of the Society who had forgone ownership of an automobile in order to spend more on autographs—asked to be relieved of his duties as the Society's secretary, which continued to be an unpaid position. He was succeeded first by John Reed, a Pennsylvania collector, then by Helen Stein.

The best news for the Society, however, was that at long last it appeared to have found a professional editor for *Manuscripts*. Greer Allen was a relatively recent graduate of Yale and a book designer for the University of Chicago Library. Books were his hobby; he and his wife did private printing at home on a small press. Allen took over the editorship in 1960 for a "salary" of $500 per issue and would be the first editor to hold that position for more than three years. Looking back on his period as editor, Allen reflected on the disparate interests reflected in the Manuscript Society:

> I welcomed becoming more central to that small universe I had heretofore watched only from the sidelines: that world where collectors, dealers and scholars met on a rather level, though subtly contentious, playing field.
>
> In this world, the collector's determination to amass material unnoticed collides with natural yearnings to have accomplishments recognized and *amour propre* nurtured. It's a world where dealers must know just who is searching for what items and in which one must gain a fair return for one's efforts and investments. And then there are the scholars, eager for first access to the material and whose hand-maidens, the collections librarians, are desperate to make certain that the material finds its way onto their shelves.[3]

Allen quickly worked out what became the standard format for *Manuscripts*. A typical issue began with three or four articles, followed by the Collector's Showcase, which featured brief pieces commenting on an important autograph, often with an illustration of the item in question. As the Society did not yet publish a newsletter, the final pages included news notes, address changes, and the President's Page. The covers of the journal became far more varied as Allen's wife, Sue, herself a publications professional, designed cover illustrations related to the journal's contents. Because of his limited backlog of collector-oriented articles, Allen was on occasion reduced to expedients, such as reprinting an entire article from *Library Trends*. Nevertheless, the minutes for a 1964 board meeting included a sentence that would have been unthinkable a few years before: "The general consensus of [the board] was that the journal is excellent."[4]

In April 1961 the charter member Forest Sweet died unexpectedly. Sweet had become annoyed at the Society's change in emphasis away from the private collector and at the accompanying name change. But David Coblentz spoke for many when he wrote to Herbert Klingelhofer, "I am indeed sorry to hear of Forest Sweet's passing. He was like a big ol' growly bear, and his ability to speak and write boldly without fear of whose steps he was tramping on will be missed by our Society."[5]

In 1950 and 1951 the Society had held back-to-back annual meetings in Washington, D.C., and New York City that were judged especially success-ful. A decade later, meetings in the same two cities would be similarly acclaimed.

The four-day 1962 meeting in New York City and Westchester County drew 150 attendees, the largest number for any convention up to that time. A morning at the Columbia University library was followed by a panel on bidding at auction. The timing of the panel was particularly appropriate, for the convention coincided with an auction at Parke-Bernet that produced $3,000 for the Society. A Society director, Robert Metzdorf, who had moved from the Yale University Library to Parke-Bernet, timed one of the gallery's regular sales to coincide with the Manuscript Society convention.

The last day of the meeting saw two busloads of participants embark on a tour of neighboring Westchester County. The first stop was the John Jay House at Katonah, where the curator, Lewis C. Rubenstein, showed Society members through the house and museum. After lunch the members visited the farm of Henry A. Wallace, the controversial former vice president of the United States. Wallace met the members in front of his farmhouse and discussed the agricultural experimentation that had been as much his life's work as politics:

My political history might lead you to think that I much prefer to look ahead than to the past, and that's generally true. But through research in manuscripts we have reconstructed the history of the edible strawberry, from its discovery by a French explorer in 1714 . . . among the Chilean Indians through its various crosses in Europe and North America.[6]

Wallace led the group through his chicken houses and cornfields, pro-viding a running commentary as he went. "I think of Henry Thoreau. . . . How far will the machine stand between man and the growing plant? . . .

There is no real substitute for a farmer who goes out in the field to look at his crop."[7]

The Society's most successful meetings usually owed much to the energy and drive of a primary organizer. In New York, Richard Maass had filled this role; the following year, in Washington, the principal organizer would be Herbert Klingelhofer.

The 1963 meeting included visits to the White House, the Smithsonian Institution, and the National Archives. At a luncheon stop on Capitol Hill, Senator Ralph Yarborough of Texas, himself a collector, discussed "The Big Ones That Got Away." Society member Gerald Carson, author of the well-reviewed *Social History of Bourbon*, spoke at a dinner at the Army and Navy Club. "It takes a powerful lot of sour mash whiskey to run the government in a big country like ours," Carson observed. "The District of Columbia today drinks more bonded bourbon per capita than does Kentucky, and about seven times the [quantity] required to slake the legal thirst of Alabama."[8]

In recognition of the Civil War centennial, in 1963 Klingelhofer arranged a reading of letters of prominent Civil War generals by their descendants at the Library of Congress. In a meeting that was open to the public, Ulysses S. Grant III, Captain J.E.B. Stuart IV, and Pierre G. T. Beauregard, among others, read carefully chosen letters penned during the war by their famous ancestors. Perhaps the most moving letter was one written by the first "Jeb" Stuart to the mother of Major Channing Price, a staff officer who had been killed in action:

Let me share with you the deep grief for the fate of your dear boy, whose loss to me is scarcely less than to you. Let me share with you, the fond recollection of his most noble qualities, and the sincere prayer that this sad affliction may be sanctified to our eternal welfare.

The dear boy fell at my side, displaying the same devotion to duty, and abnegation of self which signalized his whole career. As an Adjt. General he had no superior and his reputation as an able and efficient staff officer had already spread through the Army. . . . He was most favorably known to Gen. Lee, who knew and appreciated his worth. His career, though brief, was so spotless and successful that it is well to consider whether, amid the mutations of human events, it is not better to have a career ended nobly, as his was, than to risk the fluctuations of fortune in an uncertain future.[9]

The substantive issue that came in for the most extensive discussion at Washington was the marking of autographs, most often by means of a discreet rubber stamp. (One of the Society's charter members, Max Thorek, had been noted for his practice of stamping—and none too discreetly—

every item in his collection.) Both private collectors and institutional representatives participated in a stimulating panel.

New York collector Nat Stein took a dim view of stamping, calling it akin to vandalism. He characterized himself as "but the temporary custodian" of the letters and documents in his collection and maintained that it was his responsibility to see that they passed on to the next generation in as fine condition as that in which he found them. Stein conceded only that a small blind stamp might be acceptable.

Justin Turner took the opposite view, calling an unmarked document "an invitation to thievery." Noting that European institutions had long been marking their collections, Turner argued that marking would assist dealers and institutions in detecting stolen material. He also cited an instance in which autographs that he had lent for an exhibit had inadvertently been filed with the host institution's own holdings. The fact that Turner's autographs were marked had facilitated their recovery.

David Mearns set forth the Library of Congress's position on marking:

The Library of Congress is stamping its manuscript collections to deter theft, and it works! Because we mark, we have had stolen material returned to us. . . . With public collections, marking is important because the papers cannot be protected; we know that trusted people have stolen. But papers in private collections, if guarded carefully, need have no mark.[10]

Veteran members of the Society ranked the Washington meeting with the most interesting and stimulating that they had attended. President David Coblentz received "a flood" of mail from people who had attended the meeting, who were "happy, thrilled, and openly frank in their praise" of how the local committee had handled the program.[11] Washington would be a tough act to follow.

CHAPTER 7

The Winds of Change

For a generation of collectors, the bookshelf on autographs had been a thin one. The most respected single volume was probably Mary Benjamin's *Autographs: A Key to Collecting*, published in 1946. Thomas F. Madigan's earlier *Word Shadows of the Great* also had its devotees. Both books were dealer overviews of collecting that focused primarily on the various areas of specialization available to collectors. The autograph collector's library certainly could not compare with the huge literature on philately, which included books and monographs on even obscure collecting specialties.

In 1961, a New York City dealer, Charles Hamilton, published *Collecting Autographs and Manuscripts*, which was by far the most accessible book on autographs up to that time. It considered all the traditional areas of collecting—Signers of the Declaration of Independence, U.S. presidents, royalty, literature—and included several hundred illustrations. But the author at times appeared restless with these specialties and enthusiastically pressed his "modernist" views on a young visitor who had asked him what to collect:

> If you want to form an interesting historic collection, why not pick the Spanish-American War? The colorful personalities, like Theodore Roosevelt and Admiral Dewey and Captain Hobson, are very inexpensive. . . .
>
> Or why not go in for American financiers? Jay Gould, Commodore Vanderbilt, James Fisk, John Jacob Astor—all of them are moderately priced. To add a little zest, you will find it hard to get John D. Rockefeller Sr. and Henry Ford.
>
> Or you might try African explorers. For the price of a fine letter of Washington, you can assemble a complete collection of the heroes of the Dark Continent, including the scarcest and most desirable, Dr. David Livingstone.[1]

Such advice was a harbinger of the changes about to hit the autograph world. First, there was geographic change. For decades the Greater New

York area had been the center for autographs. In the early 1960s, however, two aggressive young dealers, Kenneth Rendell and Paul Richards, began operations in the Boston suburbs. Soon that area became as important in terms of dealerships as New York.

Then, almost as if to counter this threat, Charles Hamilton made a move that revolutionized the autograph market. Virtually abandoning his earlier retail business, he began to hold regular autograph auctions, with about six per year, starting in 1962.

Autograph auctions were nothing new, of course; the major New York City galleries had held them periodically. But galleries like Parke-Bernet were particular as to what they would handle, and irregular in their timing. Hamilton would handle almost anything—he had a special interest in autographs of the entertainment world—and a gift for self-promotion. Most important, his sales were so regular that they provided stability and liquidity to the buying and selling of autographs. Previously, an autograph, like a new car, lost half its value the moment the purchaser left the dealer's office. Now, collectors were assured of purchasing at a competitive price and had a ready means of disposing of duplicate or unwanted items.

Hamilton soon became a driving force in the autograph world. The 1966–67 auction season, during which Hamilton sold the collection of a distinguished collector, Lucius S. Ruder, rewrote the book on autograph prices. Napoleon's abdication, signed at Fontainebleau on April 12, 1814, went for $15,000. An orderly book from the American Revolution sold for $5,100.[2]

Hamilton introduced to the world of autographs a zest for controversy unlike anything seen before. He delighted in dealing in Nazi material, a category that many collectors spurned altogether. And whereas dealers had occasionally dealt in autographs of living celebrities, these became a staple of Hamilton sales. When, in 1965, the Secret Service demanded the return of a Jacqueline Kennedy letter that had been consigned for sale, the result was a publicity bonanza that left some observers with a bad taste in their mouth.[3] Gordon Banks, who was then covering auction trends for *Manuscripts*, wrote:

> The first sale this fall by Hamilton was more of a circus than a sedate auction. Unless you had considerable interest in the letters of [Lee Harvey] Oswald and Jacqueline Kennedy it was tiresome to have the sale start in the middle (to serve the television people) and then wait through a half hour of intermission while buyers and others were interviewed.[4]

Nat Stein, who at that time edited the Presidential Showcase for *Manuscripts*, questioned the propriety of the public sale of letters of contemporary presidents and first ladies, and invited reader comment. Mary Benjamin was one of those opposed to publicizing the letters of a living person:

Mrs. Kennedy has had a great tragedy in her life. I am sure that I voice the sentiments of many when I venture the opinion that she should be left alone and permitted the privacy she so longs for.

In my 41 years of experience I have never hesitated to handle letters of living persons. Most dealers do. But it has invariably been my policy to avoid giving publicity to such letters. . . . I especially avoid publication of the contents of a letter in cases where I know that the writer shrinks from publicity.[5]

In printing this letter, Society president Stuart Schimmel commented that he himself regarded Hamilton's handling of Mrs. Kennedy's letters as "nauseating." He added, "Getting a good price for your merchandise is a normal business procedure, but . . . there should be some taste shown, some sense of responsibility."[6] Not surprisingly, relations between Hamilton and the conservative Manuscript Society would often be testy.

Even for collectors, autographs were no longer only a hobby; they shared many aspects of a purchase in the stock market. Writing in 1965, Benjamin noted that in 40 years as a dealer, "I never recall until very recently" being asked about autographs as an investment. Her response to such queries, even in 1965, was cautious:

If you are thinking purely in terms of a monetary investment, I must answer: No—*unless* you plan to hold on to what you acquire for at least 20 years. You *may* double or treble your money on some items within much less time—even in two or three years—but this is the exception, not the rule.[7]

Rising prices were, of course, a two-edged sword. The collector gained a warm feeling from the thought that the William Howard Taft document for which he had paid $5 was now going for $40. But for all except the most affluent collectors, rising prices put a limit on likely acquisitions. These prices also inhibited the friendly trades that had marked the early years of the Manuscript Society. Equitable swaps were not easy to arrange when large sums were involved.

In the early 1960s, questions of authenticity, especially in the area of contemporary autographs, came to the fore. An article by Gordon Banks in the *Boston Globe Magazine* of April 1963 included the statement "Many of President Kennedy's signatures have been challenged, and some seem to be the 'authorized' variety—signatures written by a secretary, but not so marked."[8] Justin Turner, a veteran presidential collector, began checking rumors of a signature-signing machine being marketed just outside the nation's capital. His letter to the International Autopen Company prompted the following reply from the firm's general manager:

Autopen reproduces your signature with pen and ink automatically, using your own fountain pen if you so desire.

Depending upon the individual signature, Autopen signs as many as 3,000 signatures in an eight-hour day and will execute any particular personal characteristics of your signature. . . .

The Model 50 Autopen is priced at $975.00, f.o.b. Washington, D.C.[9]

Mechanical and Electronic Signatures

Unfortunately for autograph collectors and dealers alike, automation has brought a major curse to the hobby: the mechanical and electronic signature-signing devices. These faceless, mechanical robots are capable of reproducing thousands of "signatures" a day.

"A fountain pen come to life" is the description of the Autopen by its manufacturer, the International Autopen Company of Arlington, Virginia. This machine can turn out as many as 3,000 signatures in an eight-hour day from a "master" signature on a matrix, each a reasonably exact reproduction of the original. At its lowest speed the robot signs about as fast as the average person; at top speed, it signs twice as fast as any human.

Documents signed with a person's first name are created by the operator's halting the Autopen after the first name is written, thus dropping the last name. Even initials have been reproduced as patterns. Some collectors will claim that an item is genuinely signed because a ballpoint pen was used; others will claim that felt-tip pen signatures are real. But the Autopen will accommodate almost any writing instrument. Although the pattern for each signature is basically identical, minor differences between signatures made from the same matrix are produced if, say, the operator jostles the matrix.

According to the International Autopen Company, a robot signature is "as legal as though you had signed the paper yourself." This may be the case; the Supreme Court of North Carolina held in 1976 that the mechanically reproduced signature of a state official on a document was acceptable in place of a genuine signature.* Federal officials employ mechanical (and clerical) signatures on a variety of official documents.

But questions remain. What if documents are "signed" in a person's name after his death, as John F. Kennedy's staff had done? What if an operator uses an authorized Autopen matrix fraudulently? Mechanical signatures have implications that go beyond autograph collecting.

—*H. Keith Thompson*

* *State* vs. *Watts,* 289 N.C. 445, 222 S.E. 2nd 389 (1976).

The era of machine signatures had arrived. Two years after Banks's article in the *Globe*, Hamilton published a monograph, *The Robot That Helped to Make a President*, which demonstrated beyond serious challenge not only that several secretaries had signed for Kennedy but also that the Autopen had been used to sign most of Kennedy's correspondence after 1957. Nat Stein wrote in *Manuscripts*, "With the explosive discovery of President Kennedy's wide and indiscriminate use of . . . machine and amanuenses' signatures, his genuine autograph letters are gradually spiralling to prices that match the going values of Jefferson, Washington, and Adams."[10]

Looking back on the 1960s three decades later, Joseph Rubinfine, a Florida dealer, saw the leading dealers as a positive influence in the market:

Whatever the influential forces in the careers of the autograph dealers . . . there can be no question that they were, as a group, a most positive influence on a generation of successors. The work of Mary Benjamin, Charles Hamilton, Gordon Banks, and the great majority of their . . . smaller scale competitors can be considered the foundation upon which later considerable growth in the field was based.

Characteristic of these dealers was the exceptional regularity of their catalogues, almost invariably containing a wide variety of interesting autographs. Common to almost all of them were such attributes as honesty, sincerity, service to their customers, an unselfish willingness to help beginners, and a high concern for authenticity. All of this made autograph collecting grow. . . . Most business was still conducted through the mail, in contrast to later, when the telephone might account for 90 to 100 percent of dealer catalogue orders.

Rubinfine had warm recollections of most of his dealer colleagues, several of whom were active in the Manuscript Society:

Mary Benjamin's reputation and knowledge had made her the model to be emulated, at a time when women in business were still considered rather unusual. A neophyte would remember two-inch-thick stacks of signed cards by Generals Sherman and Sheridan, a full file drawer of Confederate generals, and so on.

Deserving of special mention is the work of Gordon Banks at Goodspeed's in Boston, a pillar of the early Manuscript Society and one of the most respected dealers ever. Goodspeed's shop windows, with those of Hamilton in New York, started the autograph fascination for more collectors than anyone knows.

While the major firms were highly regular in producing catalogues, other dealers were even more predictable at the mail box. Julia Sweet Newman in Michigan continued a family tradition with her interesting offerings. Paul F. Hoag in New England sold many presidential autographs through his lists. He had a source for presidential warrants and was something of a distributor for them. No collector would want 10 U.S. Grant pardon warrants, even at $6.50 each, but Paul Hoag could and did supply them to other dealers.

The real kings of dependable catalogue publication, however, were two men who seemed almost direct opposites. Dr. Milton Kronovet, a gruff New Yorker who was prone to rub non–New Yorkers the wrong way, was in reality an unselfish man who did much for autograph collecting. A mild-mannered and extremely soft-spoken Texan, Conway Barker, maintained a huge stock from which he helped quite a few dealers get started. He and Dr. Kronovet both catered to collectors with limited funds.[11]

Not all dealers, of course, were pillars of the collecting community. During the 1960s, word circulated quietly among veteran collectors that a visit to their homes by a certain midwestern dealer often coincided with the disappearance of valuable autographs. After one Manuscript Society gathering, the dealer in question asked Dolly and Richie Maass whether he could spend the night at their home before heading to New England. Richie told him that he was welcome to stay at the Maass residence, but Dolly began to worry. It would be easy for anyone to go from the guest bedroom to the library, where the autographs were, while she and her husband were asleep. But to reach the library a visitor had to pass through the living room. To assure that there would be no autographs missing from the Maass collections, Dolly spent the night on a sofa in the living room.[12]

The 1966 convention in Boston represented a departure from the Society's norm in two ways. First, it was held in September rather than May, and second, the person elected to succeed Stuart Schimmel as president was Ellen Shaffer of the Philadelphia Free Library, the Society's first woman president. Shaffer was a respected archivist and author whose interest in the Manuscript Society had survived some tedious board meetings. She was on record as wanting to see Society meetings more briskly run and more responsibility delegated to committees.

Meetings in the Shaffer administration would not be boring, for the Society was obliged to deal with a second replevin case. In 1960, Kenneth D. Sender, a Kansas City, Missouri, bookseller, had bought 300-odd Spanish-language documents, dated between 1697 and 1864, from the son of a onetime territorial governor of New Mexico. When Sender attempted to sell them to the New Mexico Historical Society, they were seized by state authorities, who contended that they had been improperly removed from state archives. A local court ruled in favor of the historical society.

Sender appealed to the New Mexico Supreme Court, which heard the case in 1962. Sender testified that he could not read most of the material he had purchased, but that some Spanish-speaking students had confirmed that they related to New Mexico and the Southwest. He had purchased them in good faith, and there was nothing to suggest that they were official documents. In due course the New Mexico Supreme Court ruled in Sender's favor, but the federal government then asserted a claim. A restraining order, issued in 1964, blocked return of the documents to Sender.[13]

In contrast to the situation in the earlier Lewis and Clark litigation, the papers involved in the Sender case were of little historical importance. Most were records of a small town in New Mexico, and many were fragmentary. But the legal issue was critical. The United States was contending that it had title to the archives of all areas that came under U.S. jurisdiction, even if the records in question had earlier been abandoned by foreign—in this case, Mexican—authorities. As in the Clark case, the archivist of the United States, Robert Bahmer, was at work with his "vacuum cleaner."

The Manuscript Society board, meeting in Philadelphia in February 1967, reactivated the Emergency Committee that had been dormant since the resolution of the Clark case. President Shaffer issued a statement that the Society would provide Sender's counsel with expert testimony concerning the rights of private collectors, adding:

This is not essentially a collector-archivist dispute. The Society strongly supports archives and archivists in collecting and preserving official papers within the areas of their responsibility. . . . But there must be a determination of what "archives" are and when they cease to be archives. . . .

The National Archives were not established until 1934, and there was no official repository for Government papers prior to that year. . . . The Manuscript Society [suggests] that a cutoff date be established before which the Government shall have no claim to archival papers if they have not been previously under the archival ownership of the Government and not legally relinquished by it.[14]

As in the Clark case, the Society directors sent out an appeal for funds for the defense. In addition, they underwrote expenses for a Society member, Texas attorney Paul Lutz, to attend the trial as an observer. The case was heard in the U.S. District Court, Santa Fe, on December 13, 1967, with Judge Elmo B. Hunter presiding. Two Santa Fe attorneys, John S. Catron and Thomas Donnelly, represented Sender. The Manuscript Society, in cooperation with Catron, had enlisted a specialist in archival matters, William D. Stern, as an expert witness for the defense, but Stern fell ill and was unable to attend. Sender himself would be the only witness for the defense. Lutz wrote to Ellen Shaffer, of his first impressions:

Wednesday morning was taken up with impaneling a jury of eight women and four men. From then until late Friday, the trial involved the Government's three expert witnesses. . . . The fact that Saturday and Sunday intervened between the

Government's case and the defendant's case should prove of some value to the defendant since his evidence will be fresher in the mind of the jury.[15]

The case involved three issues: whether the documents constituted public records customarily retained by governing authorities, whether the documents were actually in New Mexico at the time New Mexico became a U.S. territory, and whether the documents in question had been discarded by either Mexican or U.S. authorities.

The three government witnesses testified that the Mexican practice was to keep public documents forever. There was no evidence that the documents were in any Mexican archive at the time of the Mexican War, however, and this fact would prove crucial, because Judge Hunter accepted the government's contention that the documents could not have been legally abandoned by U.S. authorities.[16]

The Sender trial differed from the earlier Clark case in that Sender's counsel requested and obtained a trial by jury. In the course of the six-day trial, his attorneys were able to underscore Sender's long legal ordeal—the Santa Fe trial was his third court appearance—as well as the lack of credible evidence that the New Mexico documents were in any archive in 1846. Judge Hunter told the jury that in order to find for the government they must first determine that the documents were public records, and then that they were in New Mexico at the time of the U.S. occupation.[17] The jury deliberated for only an hour on December 19 before bringing in a verdict for Sender. "When the verdict was read," Catron wrote, "Sender broke down and there was many a teary eye among the lady jurors."[18]

The Sender case was a victory for private collectors but a qualified one, for Judge Hunter had implied in his instructions that abandonment of the documents by U.S. authorities would not of itself have justified a verdict in favor of the defense. The Sender jury may have looked beyond the technicalities of the case. Paul Lutz wrote in *Manuscripts*, "The jury's verdict would tend to indicate that the average juror does not feel it proper for the government to come in after decades have elapsed and try to claim title to something that an individual has purchased in good faith."[19]

One result of the case was an overture from the archivist of the United States, Robert Bahmer, to the Manuscript Society, to develop some criteria by which disputes such as the Sender case might be prevented. A meeting between the Society directors and Bahmer in the fall of 1967 developed no specific criteria but reestablished what Ellen Shaffer called "a climate of friendly relations" between the Society and the National Archives.[20]

CHAPTER 8

"A Serengeti Watering Hole"

One handicap under which the Manuscript Society had long labored was its limited appeal to novice collectors. The Society had never been "young." Its founders, though not necessarily long in tooth, were established collectors at the time the Society was born. There was general agreement on the importance of attracting new members, but the Society's programs as they evolved did not always appeal to young collectors. Annual meetings tended to be pricey, and the Society's journal was a bit learned for the rock and roll generation.

The Society had provided for low-cost student memberships since 1961, but in 1980 it listed only 10 student members. Then, over the next three years, student memberships peaked at 28, amid evidence that some of these were not bona fide students. In 1984 the student category was dropped altogether.

In November 1965 the Universal Autograph Collectors Club (UACC) was founded by a group of younger collectors in the Greater New York area. Membership boomed. The UACC made no claim to scholarship or erudition; it existed only to facilitate sales and swaps among its members. Young collectors who could not afford to collect Signers of the Declaration of Independence even if they had an interest in them found a comfortable home in the UACC. So did a new generation of young "dealers," some of whose ethics or lack thereof set them apart from the old-line professionals.

Charles Hamilton was always promoting new areas of collecting, and the country's most influential autograph auctioneer became godfather to the UACC. A new generation of collectors came to specialize in areas such as film stars, astronauts, and serial killers. Solicitation of autographs from living celebrities became an art form. David Coblentz, a Manuscript Society director, wrote to a colleague about one issue of the UACC newsletter, commenting with wonder, "It lists about 35 names of congressmen, opposite their birthdays in case one wants to write them a greeting and hopefully get a reply in return."[1] Within a couple of years the UACC had passed the Manuscript Society's membership of about 1,000, laboriously built up over two decades. The Society's directors recognized that they had a problem in attracting the younger generation, but did little to solve it beyond creating a Showcase department in *Manuscripts* aimed at novice collectors.

The Society's president, Ellen Shaffer, commenting in 1967 on the Society's upcoming twentieth anniversary, found cause for both satisfaction and concern:

> What has the Society accomplished in the past twenty years? Perhaps its major activity has been the publication of its quarterly, *Manuscripts*, whose subject matter is fresh, vigorous, and informative. . . . Its other most important activity has been the holding of annual meetings, and in this it has distinguished itself. It is hard to believe that anyone who ever attended a Manuscript Society meeting failed to enjoy himself. . . .
>
> On occasion, The Manuscript Society has exerted its influence effectively—as in the case of the Lewis and Clark papers—and it would seem that work remains to be done in settling the problem of government ownership.
>
> What will be the part played by The Manuscript Society in the coming twenty years in a world in which more and more organizations are being formed, and people have limited time to attend? That is for the *membership* to decide—not the directors of the Society alone—but *everyone*. To survive, the Society must be good, and it must have something distinctive to offer.[2]

Reflecting on this same period, the journal editor, Greer Allen, offered a less formal assessment of the Society and its members. "The Society," he wrote in 1995, "was a sort of Serengeti watering hole to which all autograph collectors, like all the animal species of the veldt, must come for sustenance. The entire spectrum of collectors [was] there at one time: the meek, the generous, the innocent, the edible, and the carnivores."[3]

Marshaling all its species, the Society staged one of its more memorable annual meetings in September 1968. Returning to the Chicago area for a third time, members took full advantage of special exhibits arranged to commemorate the Illinois sesquicentennial. At Springfield, participants viewed the original state constitution, muster rolls for Lincoln's company in the Black Hawk War, and former governor Adlai Stevenson's good-humored veto of a bill to require the leashing of cats.

At New Salem, the Manuscripters toured the village where Lincoln spent six childhood years. Most of the town's 22 structures were undergoing reconstruction, but in aggregate they succeeded in evoking the atmosphere of a frontier village. There, former Society president David Mearns delivered a dinner talk on Carl Sandburg, with whom he had long been associated. Back in Chicago, a keynote speaker was Commissioner of Internal Revenue (IRS) Sheldon S. Cohen, whose remarks on how the IRS appraised gifts of art and manuscripts were pertinent to many in the audience.

In returning to Chicago, the Society had coincidentally chosen a site that, at the time of the Democratic Convention a few months earlier, had been the scene of massive disorder. The sedate Manuscript Society gathering was a reminder of its ability to skirt political controversy and retain its identity as an apolitical affinity group, even in the turbulent 1960s.

Meanwhile, Greer Allen, who had served as editor of *Manuscripts* for nearly eight years, asked to step down for personal reasons. For a "salary" that was little more than a modest honorarium, Allen had taken a publication that had appeared on an uncertain schedule and with little quality control and turned it into a respectable quarterly. The outgoing president, Shaffer, lauded Allen's "excellent work" in providing "an informative, readable and typographically pleasing" product. The board chose as his successor Texas attorney Paul Lutz, who had acted as a legal observer for the Society at the Sender trial.[4]

In one of his first issues, Lutz himself wrote an article on proxy signatures that represented the journal's first attempt to deal with the problem most vexing to collectors. Lutz wrote to a number of senior government officials, from the White House down, asking for statements on their current practice with regard to the Autopen. Many recipients stonewalled; a White House functionary informed Lutz that no statement could be made concerning the signing practices of an incumbent president. The governor of California, Ronald Reagan, took the same position. But others, including Vice President Hubert Humphrey, explained their use of proxy signatures. Humphrey wrote:

The Federal Government is concerned primarily with the substance of a document and its relationship to Federal activities. For example, the Office of the Federal Register will accept documents for publication when they are received through normal channels and signed "in ink" by the head of a Federal agency, his proxy, or a mechanical device.[5]

Senator Ralph Yarborough of Texas, himself a Society member, looked at the problem from the perspective of a busy politician:

So many different secretaries have signed my letters in my 11 years in the Senate that it would be impossible for me to furnish a list. I have received over 40,000 letters over [one] question . . . alone. . . . It is manifestly impossible for any one person to answer all those letters.

When I first came to the Senate, I thought that each letter should be carefully read by an attorney, since I could not read them all, and I had a young attorney in my office to read and sign all the mail. After a few months he resigned, stating that he . . . desired to practice law and not just sign my name.[6]

The Society's twenty-second annual meeting, held in San Francisco in 1969, attracted 83 participants but was somewhat overshadowed by preparations for the following year. Regular dues were raised from $7.50 to $10.00, only the second such increase since the founding of the Society.

The twenty-third meeting—the first held outside the United States—took place in England. Some 80 members and guests flew from Kennedy Airport to London on the evening of October 24 and registered at the Cumberland Hotel at Marble Arch on Sunday morning, October 25. The five-day meeting, the longest yet held, was the culmination of an immense amount of work by the annual meeting chairman, Herbert Klingelhofer, assisted on the London end by dealers John Wilson, John Maggs, and Winifred Myers.

No events were scheduled for the first day, but on Monday morning the local committee led a tour to some of London's highlights, including the Charles Dickens House and the Lambeth Palace Library, which serves the archbishop of Canterbury. At the Society's business meeting, held in the great hall of the palace, Herbert Klingelhofer succeeded the Librarian of Congress, L. Quincy Mumford, as Society president.

On Tuesday the group traveled by bus to Hatfield House, the historic home of the Cecil family north of London. In one of the outbuildings, where Elizabeth I was living when she was notified of her accession to the throne, Manuscript Society members heard a panel discussion, hosted by former president Gordon Banks, on how to assemble an important collection.

The following day the group headed south to Chartwell, the home of Winston Churchill. Gordon Banks was sufficiently moved by the experience to write about it in *Manuscripts*:

> To one who has built his own house or renewed an old house . . . [visiting Chartwell] was a nostalgic experience. Churchill spotted the ancient homestead, 25 miles south of London, in 1922. The nucleus of Chartwell House was very ancient but in a shabby condition, uninhabited for a decade. One can visualize Sir Winston, feet apart, waving his cigar . . . as he plans yet another campaign of restoring or preserving the grandeur and charm of the English past.
>
> Unlike many, he did not indulge in the grand manner of elaboration. The house called Chartwell is a home elaborated only by the symbols of greatness casually laid here and there, . . . [including] a toy panda from an unidentified admirer.[7]

On Thursday, members visited first the Public Record Office in Chancery Lane, which holds most of Britain's archives, and then the British Museum. The museum director, Sir John Wolfenden, welcomed the group, characterizing his institution as a center for the documentation of human achievement. On the last day of the Society's longest meeting to date the group went to Oxford. Members strolled through the Bodleian Library, after which they scattered to view whatever parts of the venerable university most interested them.

Back in London the travelers dined in Butchers Hall, Bartholomew Close, by courtesy of the Court of the Worshipful Company of Butchers. The company's charter dated back to Henry II, and the original hall had been constructed before the great fire of 1666. Alas, this edifice had fallen victim to a flying bomb during World War II; since 1960, the company had operated out of more modern accommodations. And it was there, as the toastmaster repeatedly invited the diners to stand "to have their glasses charged," that the American visitors celebrated what most agreed had been a memorable annual meeting.

In 1969 the Manuscript Society established a Bicentennial Committee to see how the Society might best participate in the forthcoming commemoration of the bicentennial of the American Revolution. From the outset there was strong sentiment for some kind of manuscript exhibition—preferably one that would reach the maximum number of viewers. Herbert Klingelhofer, the committee chairman, sent a memorandum to the directors in 1969 that read in part:

> What we have planned is to exhibit original historical letters and documents of the Revolutionary period . . . in a mobile unit especially constructed for the purpose and sent on a carefully planned itinerary across the United States. . . . The exhibit will be accompanied by a curator-historian and a driver.
>
> In addition to placing insurance, the utmost precautions would be taken to safeguard the documents against heat, cold, moisture, dryness, jarring, fire, theft, and other hazards.[8]

The proposed exhibit represented by far the most ambitious undertaking for the Society; Klingelhofer estimated total costs for the program at $90,000. He and his committee members—James M. Goode, John Castellani, Bart Cox, and John F. Reed—began a campaign to find a foundation willing to underwrite all or part of the costs.

They found their sponsor in the Smithsonian Institution. In 1970 the Smithsonian was in the process of inaugurating its Traveling Exhibit

Service (SITES), which undertook to make up traveling exhibits of Smithsonian material and to display them in small to medium-size cities across
the country. What SITES had in mind for a variety of Smithsonian exhibits
was exactly what the Manuscript Society sought for autographs.

In September 1971, members of the Society's Bicentennial Committee
met with Dennis Gould, director of the Smithsonian's SITES program. For
all its historical ephemera, the Smithsonian was not noted for its autographs,
and Gould eagerly embraced the concept of a manuscript exhibit focused
on the American Revolution.

The arrangement as it evolved called for a year-long exhibit of selected
documents, with costs shared by the Smithsonian and the host institutions
in various cities. Over the next few years the Bicentennial Committee
invited members of the Society to lend their exceptional autograph items
for the tour. The Smithsonian's role as sponsor gave the exhibit a certain
panache, as well as an assurance of security and of expertise in display. The
committee and the Smithsonian agreed that the period to be covered was
that between the Stamp Act (1765) and Washington's election as the first
president. The intervening 23-year period was divided into nine major
phases, beginning with the reaction to the Stamp Act and ending with the
victorious military campaign that culminated at Yorktown.

Ultimately, 33 letters and documents from the collections of some 30
Society members were mounted on museum-style exhibit panels. Among
the letters featured was one in which John Hancock reacted calmly to the
news of fighting at Lexington and Concord; one from General Nathanael
Greene to his wife, deploring their separation but explaining his duty to the
Patriot cause; and one of Benedict Arnold in which the renegade soldier
solicited military appointments for himself and others as reward for their
services to the Crown.

The exhibit opened in Detroit in October 1973, and from there went to
Boise, Idaho; Kansas City, Missouri; and Chicago. By June 1974 it was in
Seattle, and from there it traveled to Anchorage, Alaska, and Jackson,
Mississippi. The initial one-year tour was extended for a second year
(donors had agreed to such an extension if the Smithsonian thought that one
was merited) and the exhibit traveled in 1974 and 1975 to Memphis,
Tennessee; Milwaukee, Wisconsin; Evansville, Indiana; Davenport, Iowa;
Raleigh, North Carolina; Portland, Oregon; and Minneapolis, Minnesota.

Different cities handled the exhibit in different ways, but most took
advantage of the Smithsonian's offer to show two color films on the
Revolution that helped put the manuscripts in some perspective. In some
places, docents wore costumes of the period. There was press coverage at
nearly every stop. A reporter for the *Evansville* [Indiana] *Press* wrote:

While some of the letters reveal patriotism and love of country, many deal with everyday problems—the inefficiencies of the troops or the lack of supplies. Problems with deserters, short-term enlistments, political feuds and extravagances of the troops were all subjects of letters.[9]

In June 1975 the Smithsonian's curator for SITES wrote to Herbert Klingelhofer that the response to the exhibit had been such that the Smithsonian wanted to extend it for a third year. By that time some of the collectors may have been eager for the return of the prize pieces that they had lent for the exhibit, but the vast majority approved the extension. By the time the program concluded, tens of thousands of Americans—many of whom had never seen an original autograph—had viewed and studied some of the finest historical documents of the American Revolution.

CHAPTER 9

The Harding Papers

One of the interesting aspects of autograph collecting, by collectors or by institutions, is determining who owns what. An autograph of any substance is both a piece of tangible property and a reflection of the writer's creative process. Attorney Leslie J. Schreyer, writing on legal aspects of autograph collecting in the Society's book *Autographs and Manuscripts: A Collector's Manual*, notes that "when a collector . . . acquires a letter or manuscript, he becomes the owner of a piece of physical property; but he does not thereby acquire the right to 'publish' the content of the letter or manuscript."[1]

The question of copyright came to the fore in the mid-1960s in connection with a new biography of President Warren G. Harding. In 1963, while working on what would be a prizewinning volume, Francis Russell made a startling discovery. On a visit to Harding's hometown of Marion, Ohio, Russell was shown more than 100 of Harding's love letters, written not to the formidable Mrs. Harding but to a comely Marion matron, Carrie Phillips.

Mrs. Phillips had died in 1960, leaving her affairs in the care of a local lawyer, Don Williamson. Until her last few years, she had lived as a recluse in a dilapidated house full of German shepherds. "The place was knee-deep in muck," Williamson recalled. "The floors were rotting out [and] some of the ceilings had fallen down." Williamson eventually placed his charge in a nursing home and began an inventory of her effects. Among them was a box of letters to Carrie from Harding, most of them love letters. Williamson recognized them as an important historical find and was reluctant to turn them over to the Harding Memorial Association lest they be destroyed.

The affair between Harding and Carrie Phillips had gone on for a decade or more, and was known to many residents of Marion. When the town was dressed in bunting during Harding's successful campaign for the presidency in 1920, one store on Main Street was notable for its absence of any decoration: the hardware store owned by Jim Phillips, Carrie's long-suffering husband. According to legend, after Harding was nominated for the presidency, the Republican Party financed an expenses-paid trip to Asia for the Phillipses, on condition that they stay away until the election was over.[2]

Williamson appears to have been favorably impressed with Francis Russell, telling him:

I do know one thing for certain, that if a President of the United States has written something—no matter what it is—it's a part of history and nobody has a right to destroy it. I'll let you see those letters, as long as you don't plan to make anything sensational out of them.[3]

After Russell examined the letters, he and Williamson considered what should be done with them. Once the Harding Memorial Association had been ruled out, the most logical repository appeared to be the Ohio Historical Society in Columbus, where the curator of manuscripts was Kenneth Duckett. Duckett was an active member of the Manuscript Society and had recently taken on the position of executive secretary. He took possession of the Harding-Phillips letters, promising secrecy to Russell and Williamson. As a precaution, he put the letters on microfilm.

Notwithstanding the need for secrecy, the trustees of the Historical Society were informed of the time bomb in its vaults. According to Russell:

The trustees were officially told that a large collection of intimate letters from Harding to another man's wife was now in the possession of the Society. The first impulse of several of the trustees was to destroy the letters at once. The lawyers present pointed out the difficulties in this, since the Society had a legal duty to preserve historical material in its custody. Also, an outsider [Russell] had already read them and made an undetermined number of notes.[4]

The historical society was in a difficult position. Not only were the Harding letters sensational in their content, they were of potential financial value to Carrie Phillips's surviving daughter. After several months of legal maneuvering, the letters were turned over to a new executor for the Carrie Phillips estate, Fred J. Milligan. Milligan told Williamson and Duckett that Williamson was not authorized to donate the letters to the Ohio Historical Society, and that the society should not have accepted them. Milligan retrieved the letters, leaving Duckett and Russell to wonder whether the correspondence would now be destroyed. Between them, they decided that the best protection for the letters might be publicity. Russell told the editors of *American Heritage* what he had found, and they in turn informed the

New York Times. The extensive publicity provided by stories of "Harding's paramour" made it less likely that the letters would quietly disappear.

Meanwhile, Duckett found himself in serious trouble. In April 1964 he informed the acting director of the Ohio Historical Society that he had copied the Harding letters on microfilm. The director ordered him to turn over the film or face suspension. The film, he said, must either be destroyed or turned over to the Harding family. Concerned that he might have exceeded his authority in copying the letters, yet uncertain that the originals would be preserved, Duckett sent his microfilm to the editors of *American Heritage*, who deposited it in a bank vault. He then informed the society's acting director that the film was no longer in his possession.

Members of the Manuscript Society were able to follow much of this story in the press. Sentiment was, predictably, very much with Duckett, and the Society contemplated passing a resolution of support. Duckett thought the timing not right and wrote as much to a Manuscript Society director:

As to preparing a board statement backing my stand in the Harding papers matter, frankly this would be a waste of time. The whole key to the story is the utter and complete contempt which my board and the administration of [the Ohio Historical Society] have for "professional" opinion.

Thank you for your interest. I deeply appreciate it. I don't think anyone . . . realizes the sheer hell I've had this past year—bucking the Establishment is rough, time-consuming and soul-searching.[5]

Fortunately, Duckett was picking up other allies. Historian Allan Nevins warned that the Ohio Historical Society would do itself irreparable harm if the Harding letters were not preserved.

The immediate threat to the letters passed, but at the request of Harding's nephew, George T. Harding, an Ohio court issued a restraining order that prohibited the copying, publication, or any other use of the Harding-Phillips correspondence. Russell held off publication of *The Shadow of Blooming Grove* for several years, hoping to be able to quote from Harding's letters, but finally published his book with great gaps in the text—gaps that in their own way were more eloquent than Harding's lovesick prose. Russell wrote in his preface:

When I first read [the letters] I felt a sense of pity for the lonely Harding; for Carrie Phillips was clearly the love of his life, and he was more loving than loved. Eventually, of course, the letters will be published as a part of history.[6]

Carrie appears to have caused her paramour considerable heartache over the years. A letter from Harding to Jim Phillips, written in 1918, reflected

Harding's concern that Carrie Phillips's strongly pro-German sentiments would get her into trouble. Harding wrote,

> Several days ago I wrote to Carrie along the lines you suggested . . . and got a reply which in substance said you run your own affairs. I rather felt my appeal very futile. I wrote her again . . . very seriously and earnestly, warning her of impending dangers. She is under the eye of Government agents, and it is highly urgent that she exercise great prudence. . . . She forgets that we are at war—hellish war—and she forgets how Germany treats those who are against the government.[7]

It now appears that Harding's love letters will be available in the year 2014. An agreement reached between the Harding heirs and *American Heritage* in 1971 called for *American Heritage* to pay $10,000 to the Harding family for the letters, which would then be donated to the Library of Congress. It was stipulated that the letters would be sealed until the year 2014, unless the Harding family were to accept an earlier date.

In a statement prepared for *Manuscripts*, Oliver Jensen, editor of *American Heritage*, wrote:

> Despite some criticism of the length of time during which the papers are to be sealed, we believe it more important that a principle has been vindicated. No public or personal papers of someone as important in our history as a President of the United States should be destroyed or buried forever. . . .
>
> Our experience in this long struggle only convinces us further of the need for enactment of a new copyright law, which will establish in some sensible way the rights of the public in the papers of important public servants.[8]

Paul Lutz, editor of *Manuscripts*, editorialized in 1972: "Again we commend those who assisted in preserving these letters for posterity. We hope their efforts and the attendant publicity will bring about the needed changes in the copyright law."[9]

The Society's stand in favor of maximum access to documentary sources commanded almost total support from the membership. A few institutional representatives of libraries had expressed mixed feelings on issues of replevin—one director had resigned at the time of the Lewis and Clark litigation—but Kenneth Duckett's action in assuring that the Harding–Carrie Phillips correspondence would be preserved, at least on film, was widely applauded within the Society.

As in the case of the Harding letters, the Manuscript Society was often a passive beneficiary of good deeds by its members. Two decades later, Philip Jones, a Connecticut collector and Society president, would play a key role in uniting the scattered papers of one of the great Virginia families, the Maurys of Albemarle County.

Prior to World War II, a descendant of the Maury family, Anne Maury Hirschfeld, put a large collection of family papers on loan to a Virginia library. Over the years she concluded that the institution in question was not giving her collection the respect it deserved, and in the 1960s she began withdrawing the papers—perhaps 1,000 items in all—and selling them in increments to a Florida dealer, Laurence Affron. As a result, the papers were scattered, a fact that later bothered Affron. Reflecting in December 1991 on his handling of the Maury collection, Affron wrote:

Had I the slightest inkling, years ago, of just what the Maury correspondence entailed, I would have strongly urged [Mrs. Hirschfeld] to offer it intact to some institution or private collector. . . . I feel badly about this, but I am aware that her feelings regarding institutional caretaking were soured.[10]

Philip Jones has long been an avid collector of Civil War material, and he was a frequent purchaser from Affron. When he learned of the existence of the Maury archive, and of its piecemeal dispersion, he urged Affron to try to keep the collection together. Jones later recalled, "I was able to acquire significant portions of the Maury collection over the years, and was struck by the interesting content."[11]

Several years later, Jones mentioned the collection to a Manuscript Society trustee, John Haskell, associate dean of the Swem Library at the College of William and Mary. Jones and Haskell worked out an arrangement under which William and Mary was able to purchase the residual Maury papers for the same price that Jones had paid several years earlier. On September 1, 1995, the college announced that it had acquired a Maury family archive of more than 700 items that would soon be open to scholars.[12]

Except for the foresight of Phil Jones, the collection would have been scattered among collectors all across the country.

The Hand-Written Word

Every manuscript was appealing and all proclaimed the intimate quality of a work written by the human hand, which brings the writer and his reader in closer touch than the intervention of any mechanical means can ever bring them. The written word is always eloquent of the person who wrote it. Far more poignant than the words of distress are the tremulous characters which Charles Dickens penned on the news of the death of his beloved sister-in-law only a few hours after the event. The neat, orderly hand of Beatrix Potter affords an interesting psychological contrast to the explosive signature of Napoleon, who frequently broke pens as he signed his name.

The written word possesses warmth; it breathes the personality of the writer. Those of us who work with manuscripts all too often take the wonder of them for granted. Sometimes we forget to communicate to others the solid satisfaction that we have found in our life with them. We forget our role as missionaries; we neglect to make converts. Today, with such means of communication as the world has never enjoyed before we have more opportunity to explore—even if we cannot always possess—this realm of manuscripts.

Also, the civilization which has brought us so many comforts has brought a threat of shortened life to some of the manuscripts in our care. The central heating which has gladdened our hearts and warmed our toes has rendered many a valuable manuscript dry and brittle and robbed its paper of its life and elasticity. Our industries and our means of transportation have filled the air with fumes which are causing the disintegration of irreplaceable writings. The collector or curator of today faces a double responsibility. He must inspire his successors with love and enthusiasm for the manuscript field and he must also study every available means to ensure the preservation of the manuscripts in his possession. Through association with his colleagues and the exchange of ideas he can learn to bear these double responsibilities gracefully and even enjoyably.

—Ellen Shaffer
Manuscripts, Spring 1967

CHAPTER 10

Triumph and Disaster

More than 100 Manuscript Society members and guests converged on New York City in October 1972 for the Society's twenty-fifth annual meeting. The program opened at the New-York Historical Society, where the director, James Heslin, gave a welcoming address. Among the organization's manuscript holdings were the papers of Secretary of the Treasury Albert Gallatin and two Revolutionary generals, Horatio Gates and Baron von Steuben. A special display for the Manuscript Society included a number of the historical society's 200 Washington letters and the log books of three vessels once commanded by John Paul Jones.

After Heslin's talk, members heard from M. A. Harris, president of Negro History Associates. Harris discussed the need to educate black scholars in matters relating to historical preservation, and thus to make the history of African Americans less dependent on their oral tradition. In Harris's view, there can be no definitive history of blacks in America until the scattered papers that bear on the African-American experience are assembled.[1]

On October 6 the group went by bus up the east bank of the Hudson to Hyde Park, the home of President Franklin D. Roosevelt. Hyde Park became the site of the first presidential library in 1939, when Roosevelt donated his papers and 16 acres of land to the nation. The library adjacent to the home was completed in 1940.

The highlight of the following day was a talk at the Grolier Club by the noted radio commentator Ben Grauer, who spoke of his role in the discovery of a forgotten manuscript dealing with the conquest of Mexico. Grauer had noted discrepancies in various editions of the notes of Bernal Diaz, a member of the Cortez expedition to Mexico, published as *The Discovery and Conquest of Mexico.* He resolved to locate the original manuscript, which was reported to be in Guatemala.

Grauer succeeded in locating the manuscript there after World War II but was dismayed to find it had badly deteriorated. On returning to the United States he discussed the matter with Librarian of Congress Archibald MacLeish, who offered to treat the manuscript if it could be sent to the Library. The Guatemalan government approved this arrangement but was overthrown in a coup before any action could be taken. After several more years of negotiations, the Diaz manuscript was brought to the United States, where it was restored and laminated and then returned to Guatemala. Those who heard Grauer's tale shared his satisfaction in the preservation of a landmark document in the history of the New World.

In September 1974 the Society staged its best-attended meeting to date, returning for a third time to Washington, D.C. The meeting was a perfect blend of autographs, sightseeing, and celebrities—the result of many days of preparatory work by a hard-working local committee consisting of Steve Carson, chairman, ably assisted by John Castellani and Herbert Klingel-hofer. With more than 250 participants registered at the Sheraton-Carlton Hotel, members spent their first morning at Anderson House, the stately headquarters of the Society of the Cincinnati, the nation's oldest patriotic order. There, the director, John Kilbourne, had arranged a special exhibition of Revolutionary manuscripts, including a number of remarkable letters by the founder of the order, George Washington.

After lunch and a business meeting at the hotel, members walked to the White House, where they made their way to the adjacent Executive Office Building. There, they were greeted by First Lady Betty Ford—a Manuscript Society first. It was one of the earliest public appearances for Mrs. Ford as first lady, for Gerald Ford had taken office only a month before in the wake of the Watergate scandal and Nixon's unprecedented resignation. Carson, who handled introductions, found Mrs. Ford "gracious but nervous."

The session that followed was reminiscent of the readings by Civil War generals in 1963. This time, descendants of 10 U.S. presidents read letters or other writings by their distinguished forebears. Most of the descendants who were invited were happy to participate, but not all. Steve Carson recalled a brief conversation with Theodore Roosevelt's termagant daughter, Alice Roosevelt Longworth:

Mrs. Longworth was one of the easiest descendants to reach. She listed herself in the public telephone book. But when I called her and explained that she could be a guest at the White House with the First Lady and only had to read a letter of her father's and comment upon it, she said, "What utter nonsense. I am glad I am too old for such a thing!" *Click.*[2]

Just days before the annual meeting, Carson was called by a White House functionary who told him that there was a problem with the Society's White House guest list. When Carson went to the White House a staff member told him that one of the presidential descendants—Francis B. Sayre Jr., dean of the National Cathedral and Woodrow Wilson's grandson—would have to be disinvited or the reception canceled. It seemed that Sayre had recently led an anti–Vietnam War protest in front of the White House. Carson passed several anxious days before he received a letter of regrets from Sayre's secretary, advising that the dean would be out of town on the day in question.[3]

That evening, Society members traveled to Mount Vernon, where the librarian, John Castellani, had arranged an after-hours tour of the mansion and the manuscript library. Cocktails on the veranda overlooking the Potomac were followed by dinner at the nearby Mount Vernon Inn. The following morning was spent at the National Archives, where there was a panel on a subject of growing interest, the question of who owns presidential papers. With President Nixon's resignation fresh in everyone's mind the topic could hardly have been more pertinent—although the answers with respect to the Nixon papers would not be found in panels but in the courts.

That afternoon, Manuscript Society members went by bus to the Virginia countryside. After lunch in Leesburg they visited Oak Hill, one of President James Monroe's two Virginia homes, which was then in private hands but open to the Society by special arrangement. Carson, then an employee of the National Trust for Historic Preservation, had arranged for the original Monroe Doctrine—the manuscript copy of Monroe's 1823 Message to Congress—to be exhibited at Oak Hill under armed guard.

On Saturday, September 7, weary but enthusiastic Manuscripters spent the morning at the Library of Congress, where they were welcomed by a past president of the Society, Librarian of Congress L. Quincy Mumford. The visitors then went to Georgetown University, where the director of special collections, George Barringer, had arranged a special manuscript exhibit. An eventful three days closed that evening with a banquet, at which a Treasury Department expert, Alwyn Cole, discussed forgeries of various kinds.

All annual meetings represent an immense amount of labor by the local arrangements committee, but the 1974 meeting may have entailed even more work than most. Steve Carson carried on an immense correspondence, particularly in arranging appearances by the presidential descendants, and received the lion's share of credit from the board for "the most successful meeting that we have ever had in the history of the Society."[4]

A Ponderable Complexity

Several times recently it has been my lot to sit in on various discussions where the question was raised: What is there to collect in the autograph field today that is available in fair quantity, good quality, and low price? No doubt the question has been asked repeatedly of autograph dealers the world over. It would seem a legitimate query on the surface, and yet if one goes poking into the matter, he is certain to find that whereas some personage or area of interest is available in fair quantity and good quality, it is not to be purchased in the low-price field. Likewise, what is to be found in the dealer's lists of modest price is generally not procured in quantity. By low or modest price I refer to manuscript material priced at fifteen dollars or less.

For those who do not have frequent opportunity to visit their favorite dealer and see material, but must rely on the dealers' periodic catalogues, let me venture a guess that the chief benefit derived by a dealer from his catalogue is often simply advertising. On receiving a catalogue, a collector rarely discovers a listed autograph that tickles his fancy, or adds to a vacant spot in his category, but it may prompt him to sit down and write the dealer for something he actually wants. In many listings a dealer feels he has done well if he manages to sell 40% of his low-priced items. Listing, printing, and postage, when set against sales, should make members more appreciative of the autograph dealer's outlook and his attempts at fair service.

In returning to the question, let's reword it: What, with the rise in prices in autographs the past decade and scarcity in some avenues of particular interest, may a collector—new or old—turn to for stimulation? From a general look at both dealer and auction catalogues, it seems that probing in the low-price market would include the theater, opera stars, U.S. congressmen and senators, minor literary figures, most botanists and physicists. More specifically, you might try forming a collection centered around P. T. Barnum, Marie Corelli, Calvin Coolidge, Booth Tarkington, John Foster Dulles, Daniel Chester French, Booker T. Washington, British prime ministers, or Civil War letters of the common foot soldier. Confederate paper money with a wide variety of signatures can be of interest. Free frank covers and address sheets, signed by U.S. presidents, senators, generals, as well as by members of the British Parliament, are also inviting areas.

—David H. Coblentz
Manuscripts, Winter 1963

In 1974 the replevin issue—often scotched but never killed—returned to the fore with a vengeance.

First in the Lewis and Clark case and subsequently in *Sender* vs. *New Mexico*, the Manuscript Society had assisted parties in replevin cases who were unknown to the Society, and had prevailed in federal court. In 1974 the Society became engaged in a third replevin action under quite different circumstances. The defendant was B. C. West Jr. (known to one and all by his initials), a soft-spoken North Carolina dealer who was a popular member of the Society. The replevining authority was the state of North Carolina, and the circumstances of the case made it appear initially less of a challenge than the actions against the Hammond family in Minnesota and Kenneth Sender in Missouri.

The autograph of William Hooper of North Carolina (1742–90) had long been considered one of the rarest among the 56 Signers of the Declaration of Independence. When examples appeared, they were often pre-Revolutionary legal documents dating from the 1760s, when Hooper "rode circuit" in North Carolina as a Crown counsel.

In 1974 a North Carolina collector, Robert Loy, consigned to the Charles Hamilton Galleries two Hooper documents that he had purchased at a local flea market. Both were legal briefs, dated 1767 and 1768, respectively, which had been executed in Salisbury, North Carolina. (There, according to local residents, many documents had been scattered when the old courthouse was torn down in about 1870.)

At Hamilton's sale, B. C. West was the successful bidder on the two Hoopers, paying a total of $800 for the pair. He listed one in his November 1974 catalogue, the other in January 1975. Subscribers to West's catalogues included North Carolina libraries and institutions, and after an interval of several weeks West was informed that the state of North Carolina claimed his two Hoopers on the grounds that title to any paper that had once been a public record remains with the state.

The threat to collectors posed by the North Carolina case seemed even more dire than that in the earlier replevin cases. Charles Hamilton estimated that of the "billions" of dollars' worth of autographs in circulation in 1975, at least half might be regarded by some as "governmental" in character.[5] Yet the West case seemed highly winnable. It was by no means clear that a government could not dispose of public records in such a manner as to give up title to them.[6] The United States did not even exist as a nation at the time the two Hooper documents were executed. And although any legal document has a quasi-official status, William Hooper was not a salaried employee as William Clark had been while an officer in the U.S. Army.

The Manuscript Society sprang into action, with Richard Maass heading up the B. C. West Defense Committee. At the October 1975 session of the Superior Court, meeting in Elizabeth City, the defense attorney, Dewey Wells, interrogated the chief witness for the state, Dr. Thornton W. Mitchell, chief of the state's Archives and Records Section. Wells asked Mitchell whether his replevin demand was in fact based on a 1935 act of the state General Assembly. Mitchell confirmed that it was and in so doing underscored the state's "vacuum cleaner" approach:

Q.   Were these documents in possession of the State when that Act became effective?

A.   I don't know.

Q.   When were they last in possession of the State?

A.   I don't know.[7]

Judge John Webb cited earlier testimony by Mitchell that the state's policy since 1903 had been to divide state documents into those that were valuable and should be preserved and those that could be discarded. He asked Mitchell whether any such procedure had been employed prior to 1903. Mitchell testified that he knew of no such guidelines.

The Superior Court ruled in West's favor, finding that the state was obliged to prove that the documents had left its possession in some irregular manner. The state appealed, however, and in 1976 the Court of Appeals reversed the earlier judgment, accepting evidence that the Hooper documents had been docketed in the King's Court. It concluded, therefore, that the documents were of a character to be retained in the custody of the sovereign, and not removed except by his authority.[8]

This time it was West's turn to appeal, and the result was a disaster. On June 13, 1977, the North Carolina Supreme Court affirmed the judgment of the Court of Appeals by a 5-to-2 vote. The majority ruled, first, that governing authorities in the United States had inherited title to public records from Britain. This ruling was in itself no surprise, and was in accord with precedent. The court ruled further, however, that any document that had at any time been part of a "public record" remains state property. With convoluted logic, the court concluded that although a state may authorize the destruction of certain records, any that survive remain the property of the state.

Bart Cox, a lawyer and collector who was also a member of the Manuscript Society's board of directors, attended the trial as a friend of the court. Cox noticed that counsel for the state consistently got away with implying—contrary to the facts of the case—that the Hooper documents had been improperly removed from state custody somewhere along the line.[9]

The dissenting justices J. William Copeland and Dan K. Moore wrote that "the state should have to carry the burden of proof that it had title to the [documents]." Copeland asked at one point, "What is peculiar about a document that distinguishes it from a chair which, let us say, once might have been in the custody of the state?" He added, "To permit the state to ride freely on the backs of private individuals and libraries who have expended their efforts and money to recover and preserve these documents and records, without any reimbursement, does not strike me as fair. The net result . . . will be to drive documents underground and out of the state."[10]

Many other people, in addition to the dissenting justices, regarded the decision as bad law. Cox wrote, "No British sovereign before the founding of the Public Record Office in 1838 forbade the discard of outdated official papers once they had served their administrative usefulness."[11] Charles Hamilton wrote to West's lawyer, Dewey Wells:

> The European market is . . . glutted with documents and letters of "governmental character" of all nations. No such claims are made in those countries as North Carolina has asserted. Documents signed by Napoleon as Emperor of France are commonly sold, here and in Europe, yet the French government does not claim them, much less some province or county.[12]

The outcome of the B. C. West case posed the most serious legal threat in this century to private owners of manuscripts with any "official" connotations. It also confronted West, the Manuscript Society, and their allies with a dilemma: Should they accept the North Carolina decision as relating only to that state, or appeal to the U.S. Supreme Court? Attorneys who were consulted were divided as to whether the Supreme Court would hear the case. Assuming that an appeal would be heard, there was the obvious risk of another adverse decision, one that would establish a precedent in all 50 states. At its annual meeting in 1976, the Society's directors voted not to appeal.

The West case was a setback for the Manuscript Society and the broader collector community alike. Because of the Lewis and Clark and Sender cases, both were accustomed to victories. In Richard Maass's assessment:

> [The] open discourse in communication and knowledge has now been dealt a damaging blow, and in the absence of both federal and state laws offsetting it, the decision in the West case will not only reverse the course toward openness . . . but may well bring about a period of underground activity in the manuscript field.[13]

The president of the Society, P. W. "Bill" Filby, wrote a black-bordered "In Memoriam" for *Manuscripts*:

The rights of the private manuscript collector and the private institutional repository of manuscripts were destroyed on June 13, 1977, when the North Carolina Supreme Court ruled that the state could take historic public documents from private owners without paying for them. R.I.P.[14]

Several years later, in a telephone interview with the *Newport News Daily Press*, West noted one immediate effect of the adverse verdict in the case that bore his name. He stated that he knew of dealers who, in the wake of the verdict, had emasculated documents so as to delete references to their place of origin.[15]

Nevertheless, the outcome in North Carolina inhibited collectors less than had been forecast. Word circulated among autograph collectors that the West case had grown out of the zealousness of an underemployed state attorney who had subsequently moved on to greater things. In a comparatively short time a variety of North Carolina material came "out of the closet." At a Parke-Bernet sale in April 1978, a lot consisting primarily of letters from General Nathanael Greene to various governors of North Carolina sold for $21,000. Legal documents by North Carolina Signers continued to appear at auction, and if some appeared undervalued, the same could be said for many of the less renowned Signers.

Autograph collecting was hard to kill.

CHAPTER 11

The Book

From the early years of the Society, some of its leaders hoped that the day would come when it might publish a truly comprehensive book on autographs—a volume that would be a "must" for the serious collector. Nothing could be done until the Society had become strong enough financially to undertake the costs of such a publishing venture.

In the fall of 1971, however, the board voted to proceed with the book project. It voted $5,000 for expenses and created a committee composed of Gordon Banks, Kenneth Rendell, and Joseph Fields to recruit an editor and begin work. The first two tasks facing the committee were to determine the scope of the book and find an editor. Much time and discussion went into determining what topics should be covered. It was finally decided that the book would consist of three sections. The first would consider fundamentals, such as the development of writing. The second, called "Rudiments of Autograph Collecting," would discuss subjects such as terminology, forgeries, preservation, and authentication. The final section, "Some Areas in Which to Collect," promised to be the most varied and perhaps the most useful. It would include chapters on areas as varied as French literary autographs, scientific and medical material, and autographs of radical reformers and Supreme Court justices.

The committee chose Edmund Berkeley Jr., the curator of manuscripts at the University of Virginia, as editor. Berkeley was an author who had written for a number of respected historical publications; he was also an archivist. He gave the project a solid knowledge of autographs from an institutional perspective, a wide range of acquaintances in the world of manuscripts, and a willingness to devote a significant amount of time to the work. The initial arrangement called for him to be compensated at the meager rate of $5 per hour.

Looking back on the book project after it had been completed, Herbert Klingelhofer, one of its earliest proponents, wrote:

> We knew that the road ahead was pebbled with difficulties and that it would be hard to sustain the ardor and enthusiasm of the beginning months. We did not foresee the length of time which would be required, nor did we imagine the degree of skepticism which emerged in unexpected quarters. But we managed to hang on.[1]

For a six-year period, no single project would take more of the Society's directors' time, or engender more distress, than the Society's first book. The archives of the Manuscript Society at Georgetown University occupy 50-odd gray Hollinger filing boxes. At times, the activities of nearly a decade can be found in a single box. At the opposite extreme, correspondence and other material growing out of the Society's decision to publish a book on autograph collecting fill three boxes by themselves.

Support for the project among board members had never been unanimous. Some thought it would be difficult for the Society to produce a book that could compete with existing volumes by Mary Benjamin and Charles Hamilton. Berkeley had never edited a book of this scope and complexity, and he would be able to devote only part of his time to the project. There was no certainty that a publisher could be found for the completed manuscript. Most daunting of all, the project assumed that more than 30 authors would commit the time to writing the chapters for which they had volunteered and complete them in a reasonable time.

On the positive side, the Society was able to line up a distinguished group of contributors. Waller Barrett, perhaps the best-known collector of his generation, agreed to write the introduction. Dealers Gordon Banks, Mary Benjamin, Kenneth Rendell, and John Wilson agreed to participate. For some subjects, the writers were preeminent in their fields: Joseph Fields wrote on confused identities, Judge Gerhard Gesell on justices of the Supreme Court, Walter Langlois on French literary autographs, and Irving Lowens on music. Some 40 chapter topics had been identified by the fall of 1972. With luck, the book promised to be the most comprehensive volume on autographs yet published.

There were many decisions to be made. Should the book mention prices, even though some of them would be outdated before publication? The decision was that prices should be included where relevant. To what extent should the book be illustrated? Berkeley and Klingelhofer decided that there should be extensive illustrations, but that the number should be left to the individual authors.

One matter not fully defined was the division of responsibility between the editor and Banks's editorial committee. During 1973 there were several instances of poor communication between Berkeley and Banks, which led Banks to resign his committee chairmanship. He wrote to Klingelhofer in November, "I am fed up with our editor. Either he does not read his letters or does not listen to telephone calls, since every time I turn around he has some new objection or is pursuing a course that we have voted against."[2] Ken Rendell, now the Society's president, offered the chairmanship of the book committee to Herbert Klingelhofer. He could not have made a better choice.

By 1974 draft chapters were beginning to flow into Berkeley's Charlottesville office. Some required considerable editing; others did not. Most contributors were pleased to be represented in the book; others were more demanding. Rendell submitted his chapter on forgeries with a caveat: "I will be very interested to hear of any criticisms of this chapter. However, I cannot agree to have it printed unless I agree with the criticisms."[3]

There were delays, some of them inevitable. Mary Benjamin wrote to Berkeley in December 1975:

My nephew reminds me that I had promised to send in my article by the end of the year. What shall I say? I have not even begun it. I have been totally and absolutely swamped since moving.[4]

The standard procedure called for each chapter to be read by the editorial board, now composed of Klingelhofer, Fields, and Rendell. One author refused to make changes desired by the editorial board. Two others withdrew from the project.

Benjamin was not the only participant who felt "swamped"; editor Berkeley found himself devoting more and more time to the book. In March 1976 he wrote to Klingelhofer that, with publication still some time away, he needed to devote more time to his own research and writing. Moreover, he could no longer work at a concessionary rate, given the time that the book was requiring. He asked that his compensation be raised from $5 to $25 per hour. Klingelhofer, who had long felt that Berkeley had set his rate unrealistically low, endorsed his request for a fivefold raise, and the Society's new president, Rodney Armstrong, concurred.

By the summer of 1976, after four years of intermittent labor, 29 of the book's proposed 40 chapters were complete. The goal—a book of some 500 pages, comprising about 125,000 words of text—was in sight. Berkeley prodded the delinquent contributors, but a hard core remained. Klingelhofer joined the editor in pressing those who were holding up the book. He wrote to one delinquent,

This is to appeal to you to please finish your long overdue chapter on the Civil War. . . . You told me two years ago that the article was three quarters finished. . . . A great many people would be *most grateful* if you'd get the chapter to Berkeley immediately.[5]

In his report to the board that September, Berkeley characterized the book project as "in good shape," although taking far longer than he had anticipated. Expenses thus far had amounted to $2,800; he estimated that editorial expenses for the completed book would total $4,300. However, if the Society were to publish the book at its own expense, there would be an additional cost of at least $4,500.[6] Berkeley ticked off a formidable number of tasks that remained:

Obtain any new authors as soon as possible; . . . obtain manuscripts from presently committed authors as soon as possible; edit these manuscripts during the fall of 1976; submit them to the editorial board for its review; review the manuscripts upon return by the board and make necessary changes; . . . assemble the complete manuscript and review it carefully to ensure consistency, etc.; have a printer's manuscript typed; while typing proceeds . . . work on illustrations and have photographs made where necessary. . . . When all material is ready in the spring of 1977, begin submitting the manuscript to publishers.[7]

The board, amid considerable grumbling, accepted Berkeley's budget, but only after deleting his proposed $875 charge for proofreading. The action was to prove penny-wise and pound-foolish.

As 1976 turned into 1977, Berkeley and Klingelhofer had still not found an author for the chapter on European historical autographs. Although there were chapters in hand on some fairly exotic topics, including writing instruments and religious manuscripts, the book could hardly claim to be comprehensive without a section on European historical material. In the end, Klingelhofer and Rendell wrote the chapter, which was listed in the table of contents as written by "Members of the Editorial Board."

Meanwhile, Berkeley had enough text in final form to begin the search for a publisher. He wrote letters of inquiry to several publishers with a literary orientation and drew an immediate expression of interest from Scribner's. On August 16, 1977, Bill Filby, who had succeeded Rodney Armstrong as the Society's president, signed a contract with Scribner's. It called for delivery of the completed manuscript by October 31, 1977, and set the royalty at $7^{1}/_{2}$ percent.

As agreed by the editor at Scribner's—Frederic C. Beil—and Society representatives, the first printing was to be of 4,000 copies, in hard cover, in a format of 6¹/₄ by 9¹/₄ inches. The book would be priced at $24.95, which meant in effect that the Society would realize slightly less than $2 from each copy sold. Assuming that the manuscript was delivered on schedule, Beil expected publication by July 1978.

Meanwhile President Filby grappled with the question of to whom the book should be dedicated. Ken Rendell, who had overseen much of the prepublication turmoil, had no doubt with respect to the dedication:

There is only one person to whom this book should be dedicated, and that is the person who created the idea of the book, who has pushed the project over many years, and who has worked extensively on editing the manuscripts. . . . This, of course, is Dr. Klingelhofer. This book would never have gotten off the ground if it were not for Herbert, and I believe every member of the Board of Directors knows that.[8]

No one was inclined to dispute this assessment, and the book was duly dedicated to Klingelhofer, "whose tenacity and purpose made it possible." But there were publication problems to the very end. Rendell insisted that he control the rights to his chapters, and that permission to reprint either his chapters or the one by his wife, Diana Rendell, not be granted without their authorization. When Scribner's learned of this caveat they called in the lawyers. Might not other authors insist on similar treatment? Scribner's required the Society to obtain from all contributors waivers allowing Scribner's to publish their chapters. Eventually, the necessary authorizations were obtained.

On December 1, 1978, publication of the book was the occasion for a reception at the Grolier Club in New York City. All contributors of chapters to the book and all Society members in the New York area were invited. Celebration was clearly in order. In the face of massive obstacles and frustrating problems, the Society had produced the most comprehensive book on autographs ever published. Rita Reif, writing in the *New York Times*, said of *Autographs and Manuscripts*:

The contributors . . . share with us tales of detecting forgeries, the identities of great collectors, the most popular areas for autograph acquirers and how handwriting among the prominent changes. . . . The essays add up to a splendid feast of fact and fiction.[9]

There were numerous other reviews, virtually all favorable. The *Rich-mond Times-Dispatch* called the book "a major contribution to the field of collecting and . . . a research tool for years to come."[10] *Library Journal* called it "a superb book" and "a truly outstanding contribution to the field of autograph and manuscript collecting."[11] John K. Knowlton wrote in the *American Archivist*, "The editors and contributors have, under the enlightened promotion of the Manuscript Society, thrown open the gates of the temple and provided a full set of . . . instructions for its upkeep and improvement."[12]

Alas, there was soon to be rain on the Society's parade. The deletion of funds for a proofreader came back to haunt the Society in its hour of rejoicing. In addition to some relatively minor typographical errors, the book had mislabeled several illustrations in such a way as to embarrass the dealers who had provided them. To Barbara McCrimmon, who had succeeded Bill Filby as president, fell the task of making amends and averting any lawsuits. She wrote in *Manuscripts*:

> The Manuscript Society extends this public apology to Mr. Christopher C. Jaeckel and to Mr. John Wilson for errors committed by the Society's editors in selecting illustrations that were published with articles written by these two gentlemen.

She then went on to identify the illustrations that had been incorrectly captioned.

> Neither Mr. Jaeckel nor Mr. Wilson may *in any way* be held responsible for the errors that led to the publication of these two illustrations as correct autographs. Mr. Jaeckel did not submit the John Adams autograph, and Mr. Wilson did not send any photographs to be published with his article. . . . The editors of the book accept full responsibility for these errors, and extend their apologies, in addition to those of the Manuscript Society, to Mr. Jaeckel and to Mr. Wilson for this egregious trespass on their reputations.[13]

Even with its errata slips, *Autographs and Manuscripts* was a sales success. Within a year most of the 4,000-book printing was sold out. Logic would have called for a second edition but fate intervened. Frederick Beil left Scribner's, and the Society failed to press his successor about a second printing. The most comprehensive book on autographs ever published soon became a rare book.

CHAPTER 12

Some Challenges of the 1970s

The 1970s were a period of trial for the Manuscript Society. Membership had settled at around 1,200, with new recruits barely covering attrition. Members who had played a positive role in the Society's formative decades were ready to pass the baton; even the second generation of active members was showing signs of wear. In the autumn of 1971 Kenneth Duckett—perhaps shell-shocked from the affair of the Harding papers—resigned as executive secretary. The Society's president, Herbert Klingelhofer, appointed Wanda M. Randall of Princeton, New Jersey, to the post, but after serving two years Randall reported that she was moving and would have to give up her work for the Society.

Ken Rendell, who succeeded Klingelhofer as president in 1972, undertook to handle the executive secretary's basic duties—the collecting of dues and enrolling of members—from his office outside Boston. In 1974, however, Audrey Arellanes of Pasadena, California, agreed to take on the post of executive secretary.

Since 1968, Paul Lutz, a Texas attorney, had served as editor of *Manuscripts*. He had maintained the format established by Greer Allen and had solicited some excellent contributions, including an extensively illustrated article on the evolution of Lincoln's handwriting by Roy P. Basler, the celebrated editor of the *Collected Works of Abraham Lincoln*. Still, Lutz was not a professional editor, nor was he a part of the scholarly network dear to the Society's institutional members. The journal did not remind them of the professional journals with which they were familiar, and the result was considerable sniping at Lutz.

At the winter board meeting in January 1976, Rendell said that he was tired of whispered complaints about the editor and brought the issue into the open. Executive Secretary Arellanes cautiously summarized the discussion that followed:

Over a prolonged period of time considerable discontent has been expressed with the physical appearance of the journal as well as the overall tone of the content. The editor has not been responsive to suggestions. . . . Recognition of the editor's dedication during the past 8 years was acknowledged . . . [as was the fact] that the journal under his editorship has improved; however, it was felt that the Society and its membership now wanted a more professional journal.[1]

The furor over the editorship was a defining moment in the history of the Society up to that time, one comparable to its change of name from the National Society of Autograph Collectors. The organization had been started by private collectors, in cooperation with a few dealers. Over the years, participation by dealers had declined and that of institutional members had increased, even though they still made up a small minority of the total membership. Now, institutional members looked over their shoulders at the UACC, whose newsletter featured long lists of Hollywood stars, with addresses to which collectors could write for autographs. Was *Manuscripts* headed down a slippery slope?

Not if the board could help it. At the 1976 meeting it voted—the count was not recorded—to replace Lutz by the end of the year. That fall it chose as his replacement Ormonde de Kay Jr., of New York City. His compensation was set at $1,000 per issue, double what Lutz had received.

De Kay brought impressive credentials to his post. A graduate of Harvard, he had been a screenwriter and a special projects editor for *Horizon*. His writings had included poems for *Atlantic* and the *New Yorker* and biographies of Andrew Jackson and Theodore Roosevelt for young readers. A mark of his tenure as editor of *Manuscripts* would be the use of interviews—a feature previously almost unknown to the journal. The Spring 1977 issue contained an interview with James Thomas Flexner, whose four-volume biography of Washington had won the National Book Prize for 1973. In the following issue the interviewee was Civil War historian Bruce Catton, now editor of *American Heritage*. Their dialogue included the following:

de Kay: I was interested to note that the *New York Times* reviewer, while he praised *A Stillness at Appomattox* to the skies, chided you gently . . . for not using quite enough primary sources in your research—specifically, letters and other manuscript material. Would you say he was justified in faulting you on that score?

Catton: I'll admit *Mr. Lincoln's Army* and *The Glory Road* were very light on manuscripts. I was learning the trade. I made a great deal of use of regimental histories, which hardly anybody had used before . . . but they weren't manuscripts. But about the time of *A Stillness at Appomattox* I began to realize what I needed. I got into the groove there, and from then on I was as deeply [into manuscripts] as anybody need be.[2]

Among de Kay's autograph acquaintances was Charles Hamilton, who was virtually the patron saint of the UACC but who had had little to do with the Manuscript Society. At de Kay's urging, Hamilton wrote an article for *Manuscripts* in which he flayed "snobbery" in autograph collecting, deploring the conventional wisdom in three areas:

1. "Signatures are not worth collecting." In Hamilton's view, signatures are eminently displayable and for this reason as likely to increase in value as any other autograph.
2. "Movie star autographs don't have permanent value." Hamilton maintained that the motion picture is a great art form and that its stars are entitled to the same respect as authors.
3. "Writing to celebrities for autographs is reprehensible." Hamilton said that he had begun his own collection by soliciting signatures, and that as a "poor youth" he could not have collected in any other way.[3]

Many Society members thought that de Kay had brought a freshness to the journal; others thought he had popularized it unduly. The minutes of the October 1978 board meeting included the following:

The editorship of *Manuscripts* was discussed at length. Two main problems seem to center on overediting of authors' manuscripts and not maintaining production schedules. As [for] other issues, the board seems to be sharply divided into groups who think the journal is fine as it is, . . . those who feel it should be more scholarly and needs better graphics, and those who feel it is "not like it used to be."[4]

In the end, the board indicated enough reservations about his stewardship that de Kay resigned after having served only two years.

The replacement announced by President Barbara McCrimmon in the summer 1979 issue of *Manuscripts* was 40-year-old David Chesnutt of the University of South Carolina. Chesnutt had majored in journalism at the University of Alabama and had subsequently earned a doctorate in history at the University of Georgia. An expert in documentary editing, he had been editor of *The Papers of Henry Laurens* since 1975. In announcing his appointment McCrimmon wrote, "In accordance with the desire of the

Board of Directors for an improved publication, Dr. Chesnutt will preside over a change in format to accent the literary aspects of the quarterly."[5] He was to make a special effort to obtain articles of lasting interest to the Society's diverse readership.

Chesnutt took over the editorship in the fall of 1979 and never looked back. Whereas de Kay had sought to rewrite the prose of some of his less literate contributors, Chesnutt employed a light pencil. He had a wide circle of acquaintances in academe that enabled him to commission articles on a variety of subjects. Although authorized to pay honoraria for substantial articles, many of his authors requested no payment. He later recalled:

Collectors are fun to work with because they take pride in their manuscripts and often become quite knowledgeable. As I read through a new story, I sometimes find a little-known piece of history that has been forgotten or simply obscured because no one looked closely at the surviving manuscripts. And the range of subject matter is astonishing. It can be as contemporary as the Beatles or as distant as the fragment of a medieval manuscript.[6]

To rid the journal of perceived trivia, the Society inaugurated a newsletter, to be published about three times a year and designed to carry announcements, dates of Society functions, and personal notices. The budget of that day offered few opportunities for creativity, but Robert McCown, manuscripts librarian at the University of Iowa, volunteered to handle it for a small stipend. The first eight-page newsletter appeared in the spring of 1980.

The effect of these actions with respect to the Society's journal was to move it onto a more conservative, scholarly path. Whether this was the appropriate direction for the Society in a time of stagnant membership is debatable. In hiring David Chesnutt, however, the Society began a friendly and extended association that would make him the most durable of all editors of *Manuscripts*. Executive Director David Smith remarked in 1995, in a tone of wonder, "In 16 years as editor, Chesnutt has never been late with a single issue!"[7]

In 1975 the Society held its annual meeting in Austin, Texas—the first time that the Society had met in the Southwest. Its host was John Jenkins, the flamboyant proprietor of a rare book and printing firm that dealt in autographs as well. Society guests were given a special tour of the bookstore and printing plant, followed by a buffet dinner. Years later, Paul Lutz remembered this occasion as providing his first taste of bear meat.

Over the next two days Society members visited the Humanities Research Center at the University of Texas, where the superb collection of autographs—which included D. H. Lawrence's manuscript of *Lady Chatterly's Lover* and an ALS of Beethoven—appears to have impressed even those Manuscripters who assumed that there was little culture to be found between America's two coasts. The following day was divided between the LBJ Library and the Eugene C. Barker Texas History Center. At the latter, the director, Chester V. Kielman, discussed the Texas collection, the oldest special collection at the university. Most Society members gave the Austin meeting high marks, but within a few years they would be reading about their late host, John Jenkins, in a controversial context.

In 1978 the Society held its annual meeting in Ottawa, Canada—the first time it had convened in that country. Robert Gordon, chief of the manuscripts division of the Archives of Canada, was in charge of local arrangements. Gordon succeeded in engaging as the banquet speaker John George Diefenbaker, who had served as prime minister from 1958 to 1963. The 82-year-old Diefenbaker, himself an autograph collector, was by far the most prestigious political figure to appear before the Society, but he came close to canceling.

In the early months of 1978 the press reported that the former prime minister's health was failing, and aides asked that he be released from his commitment to speak to the Society. The problem for Gordon and his colleagues, however, was that they could not hope to find so prominent a speaker as substitute on short notice. The committee expressed the hope that Diefenbaker would be able to keep his commitment. He did, and the rather small gathering of Society members was not disappointed. In Gordon's recollection:

After a dinner of chicken Kiev, he treated our members to fascinating accounts of humorous encounters with an array of celebrities of the stature of Sir Winston Churchill, Eleanor and Franklin Roosevelt, Charles de Gaulle, Harry Truman, Dwight D. Eisenhower, Pandit Nehru, Queen Elizabeth II, and John F. Kennedy. He was equally ebullient when reminiscing about his Canadian compatriots, among them his great hero, Sir John A. Macdonald, the country's first prime minister.[8]

Gordon noticed that the speaker hardly touched his own dinner, and that he appeared tired after delivering his remarks. He was quiet as the Gordons drove him home that evening and looked unwell as he said his good-byes. He died several months later, leaving Gordon to wonder whether his life might have been prolonged had he not honored his commitment to the Manuscript Society.

The problem of theft was not a new one in the world of autographs. With crime rates increasing in many areas of life, and the cash value of good autographs in a seemingly endless upward spiral, the problem of dealing with theft took on increasing importance in the 1970s.

The problem was especially acute for institutions. It was often physically impossible for a library or museum to catalogue the hundreds of thousands of individual items in its collections. Moreover, whereas private collectors were under no obligation to show their collections to anyone, an institution could not be so selective. Not surprisingly, libraries became favorite targets for autograph thieves, whose actions were not always discovered by the target institution and, if discovered, were not always reported to the police. Libraries at that time did not like to acknowledge security problems or encourage copycats.

In 1987, relatives of a donor asked curators at the University of Oregon to allow them to see certain papers relating to the settlement of Oregon. When the curators went to the files they discovered that 20 linear feet of manuscript material—papers covering the early settlement of Oregon between 1840 and 1870—was missing. The Oregon material represented but a fraction of the loot taken by Stephen Blumberg, the most successful rare book thief of modern times. Testifying at Blumberg's trial, the curator of the university's special collections, Fraser Cocks, said of the early Oregon manuscripts, "These materials constitute the information from which histories are written."[9]

In an article for *Manuscripts*, Edmund Berkeley Jr., the curator of manuscripts at the University of Virginia and editor of the Society's first book, called attention to a new program for the recovery of "lost" documents:

> Knowing that most collectors and dealers . . . are concerned by the wave of thefts threatening [America's documentary] heritage, archivists hope to enlist collectors and dealers in the fight against this menace. Led by the Society of American Archivists, professionals are taking steps. . . .
>
> Using forms provided by the Archival Security Program office of SAA, [one] may register individual letters, documents, manuscripts, or groups of material of this type which are missing.[10]

Although concern about theft was common to all segments of the collecting community, the problem exposed differences between some archivists and dealers. At the 1977 annual meeting, a former Society president, Ken Rendell, delivered a talk on archival security that included a sharp rebuke to many institutions. In Rendell's view, a major problem in

countering thefts was the lack of communication and understanding between dealers and archivists. All too often, he suggested, institutions were
too embarrassed by thefts to notify the dealer community of their losses.

A substantial number of archivists do live in an unrealistic world, disbelieving
that manuscripts can be stolen from their care. In numerous situations manuscript
dealers have telephoned institutions concerning material they were being offered
only to be told that it would be impossible for anyone to remove anything from the
archives. . . . Recently we were offered a document of major national importance
to a European country, and knowing that the national library of the country owned
the document, I telephoned it, only to be told that no one could steal such a
document, and it was unnecessary for it to confirm current possession of the item.[11]

Nevertheless, as the number of dealers expanded—the number is always
difficult to estimate, because for every full-time dealer such as Mary
Benjamin, Ken Rendell, or Joseph Rubinfine, there are scores of part-timers
—so did the number prepared to engage in shady practices. The name of
John Jenkins, host of the Society's 1975 annual meeting, began appearing
in the press with increasing frequency.

Jenkins, by then in his 40s, had transformed a small coin shop in Austin,
Texas, into one of the best-known rare book firms in the United States. The
proprietor, though physically slight, was conceded even by friends to have
an ego "the size of Texas."[12] At times he affected cowboy boots and a
Stetson, making for an incongruous flamboyance.

Be it books or autographs, Jenkins specialized in Texas material, and
some unsettling stories arose. In 1983, Tom Taylor, an Austin bookseller,
began researching some rare Texas printings. At that time there were only
five known copies of the first printing of the Texas Declaration of Independence. Taylor uncovered 16 more, all of them fakes, and determined that
most had at one time or another been sold by the Jenkins Company.[13] Jenkins
subsequently acknowledged having sold the documents in question but
maintained that he had not recognized them as forgeries.

In the mid-1980s the Jenkins Company still claimed to be the largest
antiquarian book dealer in the world and was issuing 12 to 15 catalogues a
year. On Christmas Eve 1985, however, a fire destroyed most of the
company premises. (A wry sign in a window after the fire advertised Rare
Books—Also Medium and Well Done.) Jenkins collected on his insurance,
but rumors persisted that the fire and its aftermath had provided a timely
solution for some cash flow problems engendered by ill-advised investments in oil field equipment. A second fire, in September 1987, resulted in
additional losses; a reporter from the *Houston Post* discovered that Jenkins

had filed an insurance claim of between $250,000 and $500,000, based on the "loss" of several documents, including a first printing of the Texas Declaration of Independence, that subsequently were revealed to be forgeries.[14]

In April 1989 Jenkins's body was pulled out of the Colorado River near Austin. His money and credit cards were gone, but his gold Mercedes was still parked by the river. Death had resulted from a bullet wound to the back of the head, but no gun was found. The coroner ruled that Jenkins's death was at the hands of "a person or persons unknown." Sheriff Con Keirsey, however, was convinced that Jenkins had committed suicide:

He was a superegotistical guy and a superintelligent guy. They're not going to go out here and tell you they give up. But his esteem and his prestige and his status had diminished in the last year or so, and he couldn't live with the stigma of defeat.[15]

Many of Jenkins's friends found the suicide hypothesis improbable. "Not only was the physical evidence of [suicide] highly questionable, but . . . Johnny did not take his financial problems that seriously," writes Ken Rendell. "I recall his using the line to the effect that he owed enough money to the banks that they were his partners, not his lenders."[16]

Years after Jenkins's death, Michael Parrish, a long-time associate, still thought the suicide theory unlikely. "Anyone who knew Johnny Jenkins will tell you that he would have been the last person in the world to commit suicide," Parrish wrote. "The day prior to his death I saw him in as enthusiastic a mood as I can recall—he was nearing completion of a biography of Edward Burleson, an early Texas hero . . . Jenkins had been fascinated with for a long time." Parrish was critical of the police investigation:

Late the next afternoon I got the call that he had been killed. I had been one of the last persons to see and speak to him. But did the Sheriff bother to ask me a single question? No. He had decided to conjure up a media circus by calling it suicide—a perfect explanation for a flamboyant guy like Jenkins, and the perfect way to avoid having to investigate it as a murder—open and shut.[17]

At the time of his death, Jenkins was under investigation both for having sold forged documents and for possible involvement in the September 1987 fire. With his death these investigations ended, leaving many unanswered questions. These and related issues were addressed in a dubious "first"—an international conference on forged documents, held in Houston in November 1989 under the auspices of the University of Houston Libraries and the Rockwell Fund.

At the Houston conference, Pulitzer Prize–winning author and bookshop owner Larry McMurtry told an audience of dealers and manuscript librarians that dealers and booksellers should not defend their trade as a "gentleman's profession" but should deal with forgery as a serious crime. George A. Miles of Yale's Beinecke Library observed: "Most of us involved in the Americana trade will . . . rely upon recognized bibliographic and forensic experts to avoid fabrication and facsimile. . . . A dealer's reputation for bibliographical and technical expertise, not to mention integrity, will become as important a consideration as the titles in his stock."[18]

1948, Ann Arbor, Michigan. The founders. From left: Joseph Fields, Foreman Lebold, Allyn Ford, Frank Pleadwell, William Herzog.

1949, Princeton, N.J. From left: Boyd Stutler, Alexander Armour, Victor Hugo Paltsits.

1949, Princeton, N.J. From left: David Mearns, William Herzog, Roy Basler, Forest H. Sweet.

1951. From left: Richard Lederer, Otto O. Fischer, Justin Turner.

1959. From left: Gordon Banks, Herbert E. Klingelhofer.

September 5, 1974, The White House, Washington, D.C. Descendants of U.S. presidents are being presented to the first lady, Betty Ford, by the meeting chairman, Steven L. Carson. From left: John Augustus Washington, John B. Adams, Thomas Jefferson Eppes, William Henry Harrison Jr.

1978, Ottawa, Canada. From left: The Honorable Jules Léger (governor general of Canada), Kate and Milton Slater.

1978, Ottawa, Canada. From left: Rodney Armstrong, Hannah and H. Bart Cox, William Filby.

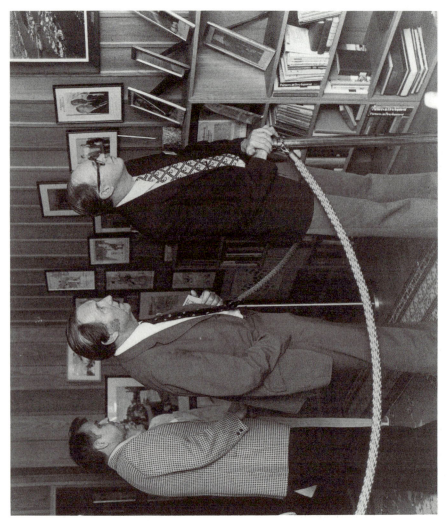

May 25, 1978, Ottawa, Canada. From left: B. C. West, Ray Rawlins, David R. Smith

1980, Baltimore, Md. From left: Priscilla and John M. Taylor, Joseph Culbertson.

1991, a boat ride on the River Shannon, Ireland. Front to back: William Coleman, Russell and Jane Price, and Doris and Norman Boas.

Five former Manuscript Society presidents pose with Mary Schlosser, president in 1981, at Clonmacnois Monastery, Ireland. From left: Philip Jones, Herbert Klingel-hofer, Richard Maass, John M. Taylor, William Coleman.

1995, Tacoma, Wash. From left: Anthony Mourek, Robert O'Neill, and David Smith.

CHAPTER 13

A New Constitution

Members of the Manuscript Society—130 strong—received a warm welcome on their arrival in New Orleans for the 1979 annual meeting. The city's reputation for history and good living also drew 13 members from Canada.

Led by their local host, Jack McGuire, Manuscripters spent their first morning at three historic properties administered by the Louisiana Historical Center. The Presbytere, built between 1794 and 1813, had galleries demonstrating various local crafts, including a remarkable exhibition of sheet music composed and published in New Orleans. The Cabildo, constructed between 1795 and 1799 to house the Spanish governing authorities, contained exhibitions relating to the exploration and settlement of Louisiana during the French, Spanish, and early American periods. A Mississippi River Gallery, containing paintings and memorabilia of the great days of the paddle wheelers, proved especially popular.

That afternoon Manuscript Society members gathered at the Royal Street headquarters of the Historic New Orleans Collection to examine broadsides, newspapers, manuscripts, prints, and maps relating to old New Orleans. After a welcome from Stanton Frazar, director of the Historic New Orleans Collection, Society members heard a panel discussion on autographs and inflation, a discussion stimulated by the fact that the rate of inflation nationally had been in double digits for much of the 1970s.

The first speaker, Pennsylvania dealer Robert Batchelder, focused on the complexity of the autograph market, but his message to collectors was upbeat:

It is my feeling that inflation will drive more people to manuscript collecting than away from it. The collecting instinct and the desire to own prevails at all economic levels. . . . Yes, there will be the frustrated collector who needs a Washington letter to complete his set. In 1960 he could have bought it for $300 to $400, while today it would be more like $3,000. He might become discouraged and drop out. But there will be many to take his place.[1]

When Batchelder was asked whether autograph prices were likely to decline in a recession, he agreed that they could fall but argued that there is usually a plateau for first-rate material. He conceded that manuscripts "in a faddish area" could be a dangerous investment but maintained that the risks can be far less than in other areas of fine arts collecting.

Wilmer Roberts, an advertising executive and collector from Philadelphia, recommended the purchase of material outside the autographic mainstream:

If you can survive, or even thrive, without swirling in . . . crowd hysteria, concentrate your activities in an area sparsely populated by collectors. Financial history, for one, is deserving of much more attention than it currently receives. . . . Transactions such as the purchases of Louisiana and Alaska and the public and private dealings of William Penn, Peter Stuyvesant, Robert Morris, and Benjamin Franklin have produced documents of dramatic significance. Yet the . . . visionaries and daring pioneers who built railroads, industries and commercial empires are, in many cases, ignored.[2]

Winston Broadfoot of the Duke University Library spoke of the financial plight of many educational institutions. His remarks would prove to be the most provocative:

With academic institutions less a factor in the market, what is pushing manuscript prices to record heights? Inflation is only part of the answer, because it doesn't account for the fact that manuscript prices are rising faster than the prices of most other commodities. I think the balance of the answer comes from the fact that there is a new kid on the block. Manuscripts are now being bought and treasured by a new breed of buyer, for their precious profit potential. To be nice about it, let's call this new person an investor, although I prefer the term speculator.

In Broadfoot's opinion, academic libraries, forced to look at costs, would have to reexamine their role in the existing autograph market:

I advocate that they should get out of the market as to the more expensive items. That conclusion follows from an understanding of the function of academic libraries. They are not museums, they are not historical societies, and they are not in the business of preserving artifacts. . . . Private academic libraries should begin to sell their valuable manuscripts, using the money to strengthen the research areas emphasized by their institutions. . . . It has been my pleasure to buy rare books and

manuscripts for the Duke University Library . . . [but] the older I get the more I
realize the future ain't what it used to be.[3]

The proposal that academic libraries consider selling some of their manuscripts prompted considerable discussion in the question period that followed.

The last day in New Orleans was highlighted by a lunch at Etienne's
restaurant, where the speaker was Stephen E. Ambrose, the noted World
War II historian and biographer of Dwight D. Eisenhower. Ambrose spoke
of his work as editor of the Eisenhower papers and went on to give his
personal impressions of the president, which were based on an association
of many years. He had found Eisenhower to be dynamic, decisive, and
honest. Ike's celebrated irregularities in syntax, Ambrose believed, were a
form of self-censorship, the result of his determination not to lapse into the
profanity he used in the company of close friends.[4]

In 1978 the board of directors had accepted the view of several members
that the Society's constitution—largely unchanged since the 1950s—should
be thoroughly revised. A committee headed by Howard Applegate undertook a complete revision and reported to the board in March 1980. Many
of the proposed changes were of little consequence; for instance, the draft
document redesignated the Society's *directors* as *trustees*. The committee
also eliminated an earlier requirement that members of the Society's regional chapters be members of the national Society as well. Other proposals,
however, were controversial, including one that called for a 21-member
rather than a 15-member board, and another that replaced the executive
secretary with a more powerful executive director.

The draft constitution drew considerable comment when circulated
among the members, and Applegate sought to address some of the differences that emerged:

The Constitution Committee reviewed carefully the following suggestions but
made no substantive changes:

1. *That all or some of the past presidents be eliminated from board
   membership.* We think that those past presidents who continue to be
   active make an important contribution to Society affairs, but more
   than half of them are inactive. The past presidents do not run the
   board or make it too large a body.
2. *That the size of the Board of Trustees be reduced.* We think that 21
   elected members is not too large and that it is a reasonable size
   permitting a variety of viewpoints within the membership at large.

3. *That trustees and vice presidents be limited to one term each.* We
   note that this practice as presently applied to trustees has not worked
   out to the satisfaction of many. We think that the constitutional
   provision allowing two terms will more than satisfy rotation requirements as well as take advantage of the talent and experience of
   trustees.[5]

The new constitution was ratified by a mail vote from the board and was
printed in the fall 1981 issue of *Manuscripts*. Some of its provisions are as
controversial today as they were in 1980. The size of the board had been an
issue almost from the Society's inception; from the 1950s onward there had
been complaints of "deadwood" on the board. Rarely were more than three
or four of the Society's committees active, and in many cases the head of a
committee was able to take care of most business. At a board meeting of
20-odd trustees, plus several past presidents, there was rarely time to do
more than listen to a succession of committee reports. The enlarged board
proved ungainly, and in May 1985 the constitution was again amended to
provide for a board of 15 trustees.

The most important change directed by the new constitution was the
creation of the post of executive director. His predecessor had been in effect
the Society's post office, sending out dues notices and keeping the minutes
of board meetings. The new constitution authorized the executive director
also to coordinate the activities of regional chapters, to be "the permanent
source of information" about the Society, and "to implement policies and
programs authorized by the Board of Trustees." Whoever was chosen to fill
this post would have responsibilities at least as great as those of the
president, whose term remained limited to two years. The executive director's compensation was set at $5,000, a $1,000 raise above what had been
paid Audrey Arellanes as executive secretary.

Meeting in Baltimore in May 1980, the board decided to offer the post
of executive director to 39-year-old David R. Smith of Burbank, California,
the director of the Walt Disney Archives. Smith had been a member of the
Manuscript Society since 1959, when he joined as a student member. He
later worked for the Library of Congress, and at the time of his selection he
had served on the board for three years and had just been elected vice
president. An active collector, he specialized in Americana, including
presidents, generals of the Civil War, and Signers of the Declaration of
Independence.[6]

The choice of Dave Smith proved to be an excellent one. He accepted
his appointment in July 1980, and at this writing continues to serve as
executive director, carrying out his responsibilities with an assurance derived from a thorough knowledge of Society affairs. He is the Society's

institutional memory, reminding the board, as required, that a seemingly promising proposal was tried in year X and found to be unworkable.

For years, Society members had considered the desirability of establishing one or more honors to be bestowed by the Society for distinguished service related to autographs. A committee headed by Bob Gordon, reporting in 1980, recommended two awards. The senior of these was the title *Fellow*, to be granted to persons for extraordinary achievements in promoting the objectives of the Society. A lesser honor, the *Award of Distinction*, was established to acknowledge specific services to the Society. In neither case was membership in the Manuscript Society a prerequisite to the award.

The first awards were made at the 1981 annual meeting in Boston. The first Fellow awards went to two prominent collectors, Herbert Klingelhofer and James A. Wilson, and to the late Gordon Banks. Audrey Arellanes received the Award of Distinction for her many years' service as executive secretary.[7]

The Society was active on other fronts. In 1979 Bill Coleman, a California collector, had suggested that the Society make a small grant to a college student working with manuscript materials in the community hosting the Society's annual meeting. The grant, which began at a modest $100, was first awarded at the meeting in Baltimore in 1980. With strong backing from Coleman, it would grow over the years to a significant amount.

To deal with the perennial problem of stagnant membership, a Member Services Committee headed by Robert Batchelder put out a promotional flier for dealers and book fairs. The committee also worked out an arrangement for an exchange of ads with the UACC's *Pen and Quill*.

In the space of a year the Society had replaced its two paid employees and added, in Bob McCown, a third. Fortunately, finances were sound; in 1980 it had some $42,000 in the bank, and a new $500 membership category—life member—promised to draw in more. One of the Society's most enthusiastic international members was an Australian, Syd Cauveren, a Qantas Airline employee who often succeeded in finding a Qantas flight to the site of the Manuscript Society annual meeting. In 1983, at San Francisco, Cauveren became the Society's tenth life member, the first from outside the United States.[8]

Two years after the Baltimore meeting, in 1982, the Society made one of its occasional excursions south of the Mason-Dixon Line to hold its annual meeting in Williamsburg, Virginia. Much of the three-day program followed the usual pattern of panel programs, interspersed with visits to local manuscript repositories. But the Williamsburg meeting proved especially popular. In addition to the charms of the town itself, there were places of interest in the nearby countryside.

The third day of the conference was dubbed "military day." Members visited the Douglas MacArthur Memorial in nearby Norfolk, where there were 11 galleries filed with MacArthur memorabilia—more than 2 million items of correspondence, reports, newspaper clippings, and photographs. From there the Manuscripters traveled to Fortress Monroe for lunch at the Officers' Club. The fortress, built between 1819 and 1834, was located on the north side of Hampton Roads and designed to control the entrance to Chesapeake Bay. It was never captured by the Confederacy during the Civil War, and Jefferson Davis was held prisoner there for two years after Appomattox.

The next stop was Yorktown, where visitors viewed the last important battlefield of the American Revolution and heard a lecture on Lafayette by Stanley J. Idzerda, the editor of Lafayette's wartime papers. Idzerda quoted Lafayette's belief that "the welfare of America is intimately connected with the happiness of all mankind; she will become the respectable and safe asylum of virtue, integrity, tolerance, equality, and a peaceful liberty."[9]

But perhaps the most popular aspect of the meeting was an eclectic display of members' autographs, housed in a small, secure building in Colonial Williamsburg. Autographs on display included colonial rarities from Joseph Fields's collection, seventeenth- century Americana from Gary Eyler, Walt Disney material exhibited by David R. Smith, and a collection of envelopes addressed to presidents of the United States from the collection of philatelist Herman Herst Jr.

Almost overlooked in the festivities was the announcement by Executive Director Smith that the Society's paid membership had reached 1,275—the first significant increase for many years.[10]

Philip D. Sang was a Chicago businessman who had made a fortune in ice cream and wholesale drugs. He was also a long-time collector of autographs, most notably in the fields of American political and military history. He rarely turned down an opportunity to acquire an autograph of quality, and at the time of his death in 1975 he owned, jointly with his wife, Elsie, the largest and most important private collection in the United States.

Elsie Sang chose to dispose of a large portion of the Sang Foundation collection through Sotheby's, and the five Sang sales over the years 1978 to 1981 constituted the most important autograph event in decades. Among the gems that went under the hammer was Lincoln's note assisting a woman whose sons desired work ("Wanting to work is so rare a want that it should be encouraged"); it went for $30,000. A rare ALS of Edgar Allan Poe sold for $8,500. One of two or three known ALSs of William Henry Harrison as president went for $28,000, and a signed copy of Robert E. Lee's farewell to the Army of Northern Virginia sold for $10,500.

The sheer volume of material was so great that cataloguing errors were common. Collectors and dealers with time to examine the material occasionally came up with remarkable finds; I myself found, in a poorly described lot of Ulysses S. Grant material, a dramatic letter directing that all sick soldiers at the Holly Springs, Mississippi, railroad depot were to be allocated space on the cars "to the exclusion of everything else." New Jersey dealer Robert Black made his share of purchases at the Sang sales but later regretted that he had not refinanced his house and bought more.

The five sales aggregated more than 1,300 lots, many of which were made up of more than one item. The return to circulation of such a volume of high-quality material was a boon to autograph collecting; collectors who had missed the auction sales were still able to purchase, through dealers, some of the best material to come on to the market for years. Even in the 1990s, catalogues would occasionally describe an item as "Ex-Sang."

Donizetti Discovery at the Royal Opera

The long-lost handwritten second act to Gaetano Donizetti's opera, *Elizabeth*, was discovered by conductor Richard Bonynge at London's Royal Opera House this past June.

Mr. Bonynge, who is also the husband of Dame Joan Sutherland, famous for her role in Donizetti's opera, *Lucia di Lammermoor*, found the score in a packet erroneously labeled "Ballet—No Use." It came to the Royal Opera in the 1860s from Her Majesty's Theater, which was destroyed by fire. "I'm always on the lookout for rare ballet scores," he said in a *New York Times* report, "and so I was rummaging through all the ballet materials" that had been saved from the fire. "Suddenly I recognized Donizetti's hand and it all fell into place. Until then I hadn't recalled that the second act was missing."

Actually, *Elizabeth* itself was only discovered in 1984 at London's Covent Garden by Will Crutchfield, a *New York Times* music critic, who also found sketches and fragments for the missing second act at the Bibliothèque Nationale in Paris. The opera has never been performed.

Elizabeth went through several stages of evolution from 1827 in Naples to a slight revision in the early 1830s to a substantial revision in French around 1840 to a later hasty adaptation into Italian. The last version was for a London performance that never went on. The first and third acts of the opera contain a large amount of unknown music from Donizetti's richest creative period. His hasty Italian adaptation was never put into final form before the composer died, and since he had sent most of it off to London, it was never found among his effects.

Manuscript Society News, Winter 1989

CHAPTER 14

The Life Member

From time immemorial there have been autograph forgers. One of the first was "Major" Byron, the self-proclaimed bastard son of the poet, who specialized in forgeries of his famous father. Then came the first in a series of unscrupulous Americans. Early collectors of Americana learned to be wary of Robert Spring and Joseph Cosey, whose artistic renditions of Washington, Franklin, and Lincoln documents caused many an unwary bargain hunter to regret a seemingly serendipitous purchase.

The forging of an autograph so as to fool a true expert has never been easy. The forger not only must learn to copy the handwriting of the person whose autograph he is creating, but must come up with paper and ink appropriate to the period. Because fresh ink applied to old paper tends to run, the forger needs more than a supply of blank leaves from old books. Dealers see enough autographs in the course of their work to become familiar with a subject's idiosyncrasies—his syntax, the type of paper he preferred, the way he folded his letters.

Nevertheless, everyone loves a bargain, and the rise in autograph prices after World War II spawned a new generation of forgers. In the world of philately, collector organizations have played a key role in authentication, but in autographs, dealers have taken the lead in the fight against forgeries. Despite the reluctance of law enforcement officials to deal with this "victimless" crime, Charles Hamilton has pursued forgers with a bulldog zeal that has led to the arrest of several. Massachusetts dealer Kenneth Rendell uses state-of-the-art equipment for the detection of forgeries.

Forgers, when challenged, often fall back on some story that paints them as innocent parties. Dealer Paul Richards has quoted one forger's disingenuous explanation:

Now relating to the fake material. On Sat. April 14, 1973, I received an unexpected visit from a Mr. George Murphy (at least that was the name he gave and which is on the bill of sale also) of Littleton, New Hampshire. . . . He said he had read my name and address in *Manuscripts* and since he was so close he thought he would drop in and offer me a few autographs.[1]

Richards did not accept this explanation. Ultimately, the person in question, Arthur Sutton, pleaded guilty to forgery and received a suspended sentence.

The Manuscript Society's role in the ongoing war against forgers has consisted largely of publicizing forgeries (as well as thefts) in the pages of its publications. In the early months of 1981, David Smith, the newly appointed executive director, was processing dues checks as members of the Society renewed their memberships for the new year. As always, there were new names as well as old. A new member, one whom Smith could not recall meeting, was Mark Hofmann, who gave the Society a Salt Lake City address.

Hofmann, who was 27 years old at the time he joined the Society, was a dark-haired Mormon who had only recently returned from two years of mission work in Britain, work that his church required of its adherents. Bookish and introverted, Hofmann had few close friends but many interests, including chemistry, history, and stamp collecting. Now he was attempting to establish himself as an autograph dealer, one specializing in documents of the Mormon church.

Notwithstanding his shyness, people tended to like Mark Hofmann. He worked all hours, and his handshake on a deal was as good as anyone else's. There were occasional rumors of bounced checks, but no one worried about Hofmann; he was, after all, a returned Mormon missionary. Had he not located and sold to the Mormon church one of the "lost" documents of the Mormon faith? The church maintains that Joseph Smith wrote the Book of Mormon from golden plates inscribed in Egyptian characters, but that the only known transcript had disappeared after being examined at Columbia University in 1820. In 1980 Hofmann took an old King James Bible to the curator of Utah State University's rare book collection and asked for help in separating two pages that had been glued together. When the pages were separated, a yellowed sheet in hieroglyphic characters was found and identified by Mormon authorities as the long-missing Anthon Transcript! Hofmann appeared dumbfounded and insisted that he wanted the church to have it.

The Mormon church paid Hofmann $5,000 for the Anthon Transcript. It was treasured by the church as a "faith-promoting document," that is, one that supports the church's version of the events surrounding its founding.

In the early 1980s Hofmann came up with additional Mormon material. He reported that he had found the earliest known Mormon document, the last known document signed by Joseph Smith, and letters that shed new light on the church in its formative years. His finds were checked by church scholars familiar with the writing of early Mormon figures. The Anthon Transcript continued to be the subject of scrutiny. After the church had bought it, archivists took it to Brigham Young University for additional tests. There it was examined under ultraviolet light for alterations and erasures, but none were found.

Not all of Hofmann's finds made good reading for the church hierarchy, for he also uncovered letters that cast doubt on the character of Joseph Smith. As a dealer, however, Hofmann was in a no-lose situation. Documents that supported church doctrine were snapped up by the church or by wealthy Mormon collectors; those that were seen as threatening to the faith also were purchased by devout Mormons—and then carefully hidden from view. Although Hofmann sold most of his documents for cash, he occasionally took blue-chip autographs in payment. As a result, he gradually developed a business in general Americana as well as Mormon autographs.

In 1982 Hofmann paid $500 to become a life member of the Manuscript Society. One year later he returned from a trip to the East Coast with a new find: a letter written by Martin Harris, one of the first converts to Mormonism. What the semiliterate Harris "wrote" made his letter a sensation. Writing from Palmyra, New York, in 1830, Harris described how he had asked Joseph Smith about rumors that he had found a "gold Bible" near his farm. According to Harris:

I take Joseph [Smith] aside & he says it is true I found it 4 years ago with my stone but only just got it because of the enchantment the old spirit come to me 3 times in the same dream & says dig up the gold but when I take it up the next morning the spirit transfigured himself from a white salamander in the bottom of the hole & struck me 3 times.[2]

The Mormon religion is based on the belief that when Joseph Smith was a 17-year-old farm boy in Palmyra, New York, the angel Moroni led him to a mountain top where he found golden plates on which were inscribed "the fullness of the everlasting Gospel," the Book of Mormon. With the aid of magic spectacles, Smith translated the text on the plates, which he described as being in Egyptian. Smith's account made no mention of white salamanders—suggestive of folk magic—and devout Mormons found Harris's letter disturbing. Mormon historians who examined the Salamander Letter were convinced of its authenticity, but church authorities also had it scrutinized by Ken Rendell, who had helped expose the forged Hitler diaries. Rendell reported that he had examined the letter under ultraviolet light. The ink "fluoresced in accordance with other inks of this period," he said, and the paper was of a type commonly used in New York State in the early nineteenth century. Rendell was handicapped by the fact that there were few known examples of Martin Harris's handwriting, but he concluded that the signature on the Salamander Letter "is consistent with three other known examples of Harris's signature."3

Hofmann sold the Salamander Letter to a devout Mormon, Steve Christensen, for $40,000. (Christensen later donated the letter to the church, lest it fall into the wrong hands.) Meanwhile, Hofmann's business continued to prosper. In 1983 he and his wife, Doralee, moved to a large home in a Salt Lake City suburb. There they entertained friends in a backyard hot tub, but Mark said little about his remarkable autograph finds.

In the spring of 1985 Hofmann confided to a few friends that he might have made his greatest discovery to date, one of interest not only to Mormons but to all Americans. He claimed to have found a legendary rarity in printing—the Oath of a Freeman, a pledge required of citizens of the Massachusetts Bay Company in the seventeenth century. The oath embodied an early expression of independence by the colonists, for the person executing it promised to "give my vote & suffrage as I shall judge in myne owne conscience . . . without respect of personnes, or favour of any man."4 Scholars believed that there had been about 50 copies of the oath, each about the size of a postcard, but none was known to have survived. Apart from its intrinsic historical interest, a genuine example of the Oath of a Freeman would be the earliest surviving example of printing in Britain's North American colonies.

According to Hofmann, the oath was a serendipitous find, tucked among a cache of old papers he had bought at the Argosy Book Store on New York's East 59th Street. As store records would verify, he had indeed bought a batch of old documents at Argosy. It was later revealed, however, that Hofmann had first created a crudely forged broadside titled *Oath of a Freeman* with a notional dealer's price of $25 on the verso. Having placed the broadside in a box of old documents at Argosy, he then purchased it, obtaining a receipt that included the spurious *Oath*. With this "provenance" in hand, Hofmann then set out to create a forgery that would fool the world.5

Ultimately, the *Oath of a Freeman* proved Hofmann's undoing. Because preliminary examinations, including one at the Library of Congress, indicated that it was genuine, Hofmann assumed that he would obtain something close to his $1.5 million asking price. He overextended himself in various areas and soon was having to stave off creditors. When the Library of

Congress told him that it was not prepared to meet his price for the oath, Hofmann spoke vaguely of acquiring a long-lost trove of Mormon documents, the McLellin Collection.

Steve Christensen, the collector who had purchased the Salamander Letter, considered Hofmann a friend, but he had lately become suspicious of some of Mark's practices, including his attempts to sell items from the McLellin Collection before he had purchased it. Did Christensen also suspect his friend's uncanny ability to generate important Mormon documents? On October 11, 1985, Christensen arrived at his office in a downtown Salt Lake City building, where he found a package addressed to him outside the door. When he picked up the box it exploded, driving metal fragments into his chest and causing death within minutes.

Across town, Kathy Sheets, the wife of one of Christensen's business associates, found a similar package outside her home. When she picked it up, it also exploded, killing her instantly. The following day, Mark Hofmann climbed into his Toyota sports car, parked near Temple Square. The explosion that followed rattled nearby windows and blew Hofmann into the street. The car was totally destroyed and Hofmann seriously but not critically injured.

Murder by bomb was sufficiently rare in Utah that the so-called Mormon murders engaged the attention of some of the ablest homicide detectives in the state. At first they assumed that Hofmann was also a victim, just luckier than the others. But his statement to police that he was outside the car when the bomb exploded was contrary to physical evidence indicating that he had been inside. This small discrepancy intrigued police, especially when officials of the Mormon church filled them in on Hofmann's extensive, sometimes devious dealings. Hofmann was added to the list of suspects, but no one could establish a motive for his killing Christensen and Kathy Sheets.

Two document experts, George Throckmorton and William Flynn, began examining Mormon documents that had been sold to the church by Hofmann. Whereas other experts who had examined Hofmann's handiwork had not been suspicious, Throckmorton and Flynn operated from a hunch that Hofmann was a forger. Eventually they noted that the ink on Hofmann's documents demonstrated, under the microscope, a crackling pattern that the ink in genuine documents of the period did not.

Hofmann spent three weeks in the hospital and, because of injuries to one knee, was discharged in a wheelchair. By then police were treating him as a suspect, and the young dealer declined to speak to reporters. But he passed a lie detector test with flying colors.

The following weeks saw a triumph of gritty police work. Seeking to link Hofmann with the mercury switches that had detonated the bombs, investigators found that they had been sold by RadioShack. Days of diligent searching through the records of several RadioShack stores were rewarded when police found a receipt for mercury switches in an alias that Hofmann was known to have used.

On February 4, 1986, Hofmann was arrested and charged with first-degree murder in the deaths of Steve Christensen and Kathy Sheets. In addition, he was charged with 23 counts of theft and fraud against a long list of victims, including the Church of Jesus Christ of Latter-day Saints. The implication that Hofmann's most famous finds in Mormon documents were forgeries produced a wave of disbelief among Mormon scholars. Prosecutors, meanwhile, were not sure of how strong a case they had against Hofmann, for his motive in the two killings remained unclear.

On January 7, 1987, Hofmann's attorney asked police officers to go to his house, saying that his client wanted to make a statement. That evening Hofmann confessed that he had carried out the bombings and that he had acted alone. He gave a detailed description of how he had constructed the bombs. According to one of the officers:

It was an amazing scene. He was very concerned about the details and he wanted to go over [them] time after time. . . .

He wanted us to know that the pipe bomb was his own construction, that he pretty well thought the thing out himself. He was very, very proud of it and even drew a diagram for us showing how really simple the pipe bombs were.[6]

Why had Hofmann killed Christensen and Sheets? He had feared that Christensen might tell his creditors that any funds Hofmann might realize from the McLellin Collection would not be used to pay old debts. As for Kathy Sheets, she was not the intended victim; Hofmann had intended to kill her husband as a diversion. To a prison psychologist Hofmann elaborated on his confession:

In October 1985, it seemed like everything started to collapse around me. I could not come up with money to pay off investors to keep from being exposed as a fraud. . . . The most important thing in my mind was to keep from being exposed as a fraud in front of my friends and family.[7]

On January 23, 1987, Hofmann pleaded guilty to second-degree murder in the deaths of Christensen and Sheets. He also admitted that the Salamander Letter was a forgery and that his attempts to sell the McLellin Collection constituted fraud. Judge Kenneth Rigtrup sentenced Hofmann to four concurrent terms of four years to life and recommended that he spend the rest of his life behind bars.[8]

Bombs aside, Mark Hofmann was probably the most dangerous forger of all time. His technical skill was remarkable; Ken Rendell thought that he "had no equal" in the creation of appropriate ink.[9] He was also capable of killing anyone who stood in his way. But he was perhaps most skilled at projecting an air of innocence. Rendell writes:

> Hofmann was a master at gaining the confidence of his victims. Even after he was charged with murder, virtually everyone who knew him could not believe him guilty. . . . While I did not know Hofmann as well as his victims, my five or six encounters with him left me with the clear opinion that he could not have been a murderer.[10]

Charles Hamilton, who admitted to having been taken in by Hofmann, put him in perspective:

> Mark Hofmann was unquestionably the most skilled forger this country has ever seen. [It was] not just because he was a good technician. He got away with it because he had a knack for making people like and trust him. He fooled me, he fooled Ken Rendell, he fooled the whole world.[11]

Interviewed for the Society's newsletter in the autumn of 1988, Rendell spoke of Hofmann with something approaching awe. "Hofmann is important because of his tremendous attention to detail," he remarked. "Forgers tend to miss something big, but not Hofmann." Of what should collectors be wary? Rendell added, with knowledge painfully acquired:

> The telltale signs of Hofmann forgeries are that they fluoresce bright blue under high intensity ultraviolet light and that the ink has the appearance of a reptile skin when it is magnified very significantly. This cracking of the ink's surface is a result of the chemical put on the ink to prevent its feathering.[12]

The Manuscript Society had long avoided becoming involved in questions of ethics among its members. Mark Hofmann's status as a life member, however, posed a problem. Although the bylaws permitted the nonrenewal of the membership of someone who had been convicted of a crime involving manuscripts, nothing was said about murder.

Fortunately, Hofmann had also confessed to forgery, a crime involving manuscripts. After a brief discussion at the 1987 annual meeting, his name was quietly dropped from the rolls.

CHAPTER 15

New Fields

Over the years, the Manuscript Society's decision-making structure had evolved from a gathering of "old hands" to a formal organization in which the chairman of the annual meeting committee—the "program chair"—loomed especially large. No position in the Society held greater potential for glory or disaster; because the annual meeting was the Society's most visible activity, the program chair could make or break the Society for a year. Archivist George Vogt, who took the job in 1980, was one in a series of fortunate choices for this key position. After leaving the program chair for the greater glory of the presidency, Vogt was moved to reminisce about the challenges and rewards of his previous position:

The meeting industry is a highly developed one which sports its own glossy, four-color trade literature. The magazines begin arriving unbidden and free of charge. Most of them consist of hotel advertisements and seductive photos shot at poolside. Very occasionally, they carry something truly useful, such as a chart showing the drinking capacity of 40 people over a three-hour period, with or without hors d'oeuvres. . . .

As I warmed to my job, it became apparent that from almost everyone's perspective, the Society's meetings are unusual. We favor the Memorial Day weekend, when everyone else is in Indianapolis; we spend very little time in "sessions" at the base hotel; we go places and do things previously unknown to most local convention bureaus; and we make astonishingly few demands on hotel staffers who are quite accustomed to arranging kosher Hawaiian luaus on three hours' notice. . . .

In four years, . . . I formulated Vogt's Laws of Meeting Planning, which I would like to share with you.

1. *There is never too much coffee.* Try omitting a coffee break during a busy morning of touring and see what happens.

2. *There is always too much food, but only the skinny people complain.*
   For economic reasons, hotels and restaurants want to serve full hot
   meals with desserts at both lunch and dinner. After three days, slim
   ladies are known to weep at the sight of another beef bourguignon
   and snatch at passing tossed salads.

3. *People who miss buses always show up.* Ergo, there is no point in
   worrying about it.

4. *There is too much or too little free time on any program.* Depending
   on the local supply of manuscript dealers, rare book shops, and art
   galleries, as well as the individual members' proclivities, the meeting planner hears both comments freely voiced every hour or so.

5. *When in doubt, hire a boat.* Trains don't do it. Buses certainly don't
   do it. A paddle-wheeler or even a party barge does it in style. The
   crankiest bunch of over-toured connoisseurs will turn into pussycats
   in 15 minutes on a boat, if there is a bar.[1]

Vogt's last hurrah as program chair was at the 1984 meeting, held for the
fourth time in the Greater New York City area, with headquarters this time
in Tarrytown. The morning of Thursday, May 24, was spent visiting Sun-
nyside, the home of author Washington Irving. There Andrew Myers, an
Irving scholar and longtime member of the Society, spoke on Irving as a
figure in the nineteenth-century world of letters. Society members then
traveled to the Rockefeller Archive Center at Pocantico Hills and to the
nearby Union Church, which has stained-glass windows by Marc Chagall.
Coffee, naturally, was available in abundance. The afternoon was divided
between Lyndhurst, the Gothic Revival mansion once occupied by railroad
baron Jay Gould, and the John Jay home at Katonah, New York. The auction
that evening was run by George Lowry of Swann Galleries. When it was
over, the auction chairman, James F. Ruddy, was able to announce that the
Society's share of the proceeds had topped $10,000 for the first time.

Friday was spent in the city proper, divided between the music library at
Lincoln Center, where members viewed manuscripts of Bach, Mozart,
Beethoven, and Brahms, and the Pierpont Morgan Library, whose collection
of music manuscripts is second only to that of the Library of Congress. The
final call that afternoon was at the New-York Historical Society, where a
special exhibition of autographs featured examples of John Winthrop,
Robert Fulton, Peter Stuyvesant, and John Jay.

The day included lunch at the Maestro Cafe and dinner at Rockefeller
Center. Not even skinny people complained.

The buses left early the next morning for the Franklin D. Roosevelt
Library and Museum at Hyde Park. There, members were greeted by the

library director, William Emerson, who spoke briefly on the history of his institution, the first presidential library. Emerson pointed out that FDR was a zealous collector for most of his life—a collector not only of stamps, for which he was renowned, but also of books, paintings, nautical art, and manuscripts.[2]

After lunch at Hyde Park, members were bussed across the Hudson to West Point, where, in conformity with Vogt's Law No. 5, members boarded the *Commander* for a two-hour cruise down the river to Haverstraw. The annual business meeting was held on board, and a grateful Society promoted Vogt from program chair to president. "There ought to be a rule about choosing the proper moment to leave your post," George later mused. "A month after I quit, a hotel chain whisked my successor to London on the *Concorde* for an arduous week of hotel and restaurant exploration."[3]

Arizona collector Ira Brilliant is not a typical Manuscript Society member. A retired real estate developer, he is prone to remark, shyly, that *his* autograph collection contains only five items. To the raised eyebrows provoked by this admission, Ira will then acknowledge that his five items are letters of Ludwig van Beethoven—arguably the greatest composer the world has known, and a very rare autograph. In 1985 Brilliant donated his Beethoven collection, together with rare first editions of Beethoven's music, to San Jose State University in California, where the Ira F. Brilliant Center for Beethoven Studies became the first in North America devoted to the composer.

While serving on the Manuscript Society board in the early 1980s, Brilliant reflected on the amount of historical material represented by the collections of his Society colleagues. In a letter to the Society's president, he advanced the idea of a manuscript database to which scholars might turn for a listing of letters concerning a person or subject of special interest. For a small fee, anyone could request a computer search on the person in question.

Most board members agreed that such a database might be useful, but then proceeded to consider the obstacles. How could the Society, run as it was by a part-time staff, take on its management? With the B. C. West replevin case fresh in members' minds, who would allow his or her prize autographs to enter any database? What assurances could the Society give participants that their ownership of a certain document would not leak? "It was slow going at first," Brilliant recalls. "I found a few converts, a lot of indifference, and some [people] flatly opposed."[4]

Ira was not discouraged. With authority from the board to look into means of meeting these problems, he visited Arizona State University, where he discussed his project with Ed Oetting, director of the department of archives and manuscripts. In 1986, the two men reached a tentative agreement under which the university would provide computers and labor to record autographs to be provided by Society members.

On November 16, 1987, President William R. Coleman of the Manuscript Society signed a contract with Arizona State University based on Brilliant's understanding with Oetting. Confidentiality was to be guaranteed by assigning each participating collector a numerical code; staff members who handled requests would not have access to information concerning a document's ownership. Brilliant recalled in 1990:

> With the system in place and the computer at ASU waiting for entries, I then went on a hunt for material. Using our annual conventions, the phone and the mails, I found about 10 members strategically located in different parts of the country and appointed them field commanders. They were each assigned a block of 200 numbers and asked to recruit participants in their geographic areas. Over half of the field commanders submitted either their entire collections or choice items. But I was not too successful in getting the commanders to get entries from others.[5]

By 1994, information on nearly 4,000 documents had been entered into the database. The staff at the university had responded to 17 requests for searches, and in all except 3 cases had been able to provide at least one item. The Western History Association published a description of the database in its spring 1994 newsletter, generating new search requests. A description of the database was put on the Internet, making it effectively a worldwide service.

The database has the potential of being the Manuscript Society's most important contribution to the use of autographs in scholarship. Although many collectors will continue to withhold some items, especially any seen as vulnerable to replevin, the database provides a means for collectors to share "content" items with students of a particular person or era. Ira Brilliant still has a dream:

> It is how I imagine the Manuscripts Database will be functioning four or five years from now. The contributors number in the hundreds, the entries total somewhere over 20,000, and the shoebox used in the beginning is long gone. . . . The database is an established resource well known to professional historians.[6]

Although the growth of the database has been slow, its potential is great. And just as publication of the Society's first book owed most to Herbert Klingelhofer, establishment of the database represented years of hard work by Ira Brilliant.

At the same time the database was getting under way, the Society undertook its second hard-cover publication, an anthology of articles from its journal *Manuscripts*. Many members had long believed that the best of the articles from the Society's journal, some of them from *Autograph Collectors' Journal*, deserved republication in more permanent form. For a time, the problems that had attended the Society's first book cooled enthusiasm for any sequel, but by 1980 the board had agreed in principle on the desirability of a *Manuscripts* anthology. An ad hoc committee composed of Herbert Klingelhofer, Ken Rendell, and John M. Taylor was set up to select the best from the Society's first 20 years.

By the end of 1981 the committee had settled on 56 articles and was ready to proceed. The board selected Priscilla Taylor, a professional editor and the wife of John M. Taylor, as editor. She was expected to organize and condense the material as necessary, update price references, and otherwise polish the products of many different writing styles.

By March 1983 the anthology was ready for publication. It was a book of remarkable variety, with subjects ranging from medieval royal autographs to tips on buying by mail, from confused identities to lottery tickets. The board had no difficulty in attracting publishers. Two, Greenwood Press and the University of Virginia Press, made offers, though both involved a subsidy from the Society. The board elected to go with Greenwood, whose terms stipulated that the Society purchase 500 of the 2,000 copies printed at the wholesale price.

Manuscripts: The First Twenty Years appeared in 1984. In contrast to *Autographs and Manuscripts*, it was free of editorial glitches, although the publisher employed a type size that was less than user-friendly. Reviews were few but favorable; the *Journal of Academic Librarianship* wrote, "Dealers, collectors, and anyone fascinated by the world of autograph collecting will find this volume a treat."[7]

Over the years, some members had regretted that the Society did not have a physical headquarters—a central office that members could visit and perhaps use for research. Such an office was difficult to arrange, in part because the Society had no full-time staff. The Burbank, California, home of Executive Director David Smith, was the Society's mailing address but could hardly serve as a central office.

In 1981 the board asked Herbert Klingelhofer to investigate the possibility of a permanent reading room for the Society. Thanks to John Mayfield, a Society member who was librarian of the Army and Navy Club in downtown Washington, D.C., the Society was given use of a room in the club at a rate of only $350 per year. Members contributed books relating to autographs and copies of dealer catalogues. Four years later, however, Mayfield died, and the Army and Navy Club underwent a renovation and a change in management. For several years the Society had no home. Although Georgetown University had agreed to house the Society's archives, no institution was in a position to offer a reading room. In 1987, however, the Society signed an arrangement with the University of Virginia. During the 1990s the Society's library was integrated with the university's own collection of manuscript-related materials.

The Society held its 1986 annual meeting in London, the second time it had convened in Britain. Although the meeting drew only 80 registrants, the seven-day program included the usual stimulating visits to institutions such as the British Library, Hatfield House in Hertfordshire, Cambridge University, and the historic Guildhall in the City. At the home of Patricia and Gerald Coke in Hampshire, members were able to view the Cokes' remarkable collection relating to George Frederic Handel, including letters, prints, concert tickets, and sheet music.

Nevertheless, the London meeting included some glitches. Although Sotheby's of London had agreed to hold a sale in conjunction with the Manuscript Society visit and Society members had consigned some $180,000 worth of material, some lots were refused at the eleventh hour and then not promptly returned to consignors. The auction chairman, Jim Ruddy, spent hours on the phone attempting to resolve this problem. The meeting was also a financial shock to the Society. The treasurer, B. C. West, told the board in October 1986 that, because of heavy startup costs, the London meeting had resulted in a deficit of about $27,000. Once the bills were paid, the Society's financial position was weaker than at any time in recent memory, with only about $27,200 left in the bank.[8]

Nevertheless, the next annual meeting, held in Washington, D.C., the following spring—the bicentennial of the Constitution—proved to be one of the most successful. Program chairman Robert O'Neill, assisted by such Washington area stalwarts as Ellen Clark, Steve Carson, Brian Richter, and Carolyn Sung, arranged a four-day program that included trips to Mount Vernon, Gunston Hall, and Monticello. A total of 214 persons—a Society record to date—attended the Washington meeting.

One of the high spots of the meeting was a visit to the National Archives, where Coretta Scott King delivered the address that marked the Archives' formal opening of the bicentennial. Speaking as the granddaughter of a slave, she said that while we celebrate the virtues of the Constitution we should not ignore the shortcomings of its framers. Fortunately, she noted, the Constitution is a flexible document, and the authorization of slavery and the disenfranchisement of women had been corrected. The bicentennial, she believed, represented an opportunity to learn how far America has come, and how far we have to go.[9]

Friday evening, Manuscripters went to the Supreme Court for the opening of a bicentennial manuscripts exhibition mounted by the Society under the leadership of Howard Goldman. Titled "Documenting the Constitution: A Manuscript History," the exhibit comprised documents relating to the framing, ratification, and interpretation of the Constitution. The exhibit consisted largely of items from the collections of Society members, including letters of Washington, Jefferson, Hamilton, and Marshall.

During the 1987 annual meeting in Washington, David Smith and Herbert Klingelhofer found themselves in adjoining seats for one of the bus trips. Their conversation eventually turned to the fact that nowhere in the literature of autographs was there a quick-reference guide to the prominent names in various collecting specialties and the rarity of their autographs. Should the Manuscript Society undertake to fill this void?

At the October 1988 board meeting, Klingelhofer, with the backing of several board members, suggested that the Society look into the possibility of publishing a book of lists as a research aid for collectors. The book would consider not only traditional collecting categories, such as presidents and cabinet members, but lesser known groups such as leaders of the War of 1812 and presidential also-rans. John M. Taylor, chairman of the Publications Committee, was named editor.

The book was titled *Autograph Collector's Checklist*, and work went forward at a brisk pace. Within a year of the board's approval, 12 authors had produced a total of 22 chapters that briefly discussed, in terms of their autographic availability, thousands of individuals from Martha Washington to Jimmy Doolittle.

The *Checklist* appeared in 1990 in a printing of 1,500, at a total cost of $14,000. The 170-page paperback was produced by the South Carolina company that prints *Manuscripts* and as such represented the Society's first publishing venture on its own. The Society itself acted as bookseller, retailing copies at $15.95; most of the initial investment was recovered within three years.

CHAPTER 16

The Society in the 1990s

The October 1990 meeting of the Manuscript Society board, held at the Folger Library in Washington, D.C., opened as usual with David Smith's report as executive director. Smith reported a total membership of 1,528, an increase of 4 percent over the previous year's total. Of this total, 1,311 were individual members and 217 were institutions. The treasurer, Howard Goldman, reported net assets of slightly more than $80,000, a remarkable comeback from the $27,000 of four years previous. Three factors—the generosity of individual "angels," the growing number of life members, and proceeds from the annual auctions—had restored the Society's finances.[1]

The Society's growth reflected nonfinancial factors as well. Under Steve Carson's editorship, the newsletter had expanded from 8 pages to 35 pages or more, covering a wide variety of stories related to autographs. David Chesnutt continued to attract a stimulating variety of writers for *Manuscripts*. The 1980s had seen articles such as Ralph H. Orth's "Editing Emerson's Poetry Notebooks"; Ralph D. Gardner's authoritative discussion of writer Horatio Alger; and special issues devoted to Lincoln and to the Constitution's bicentennial. A two-part article by Penne Laingen, retelling the 1979 Iran hostage crisis through the letters of her husband, imprisoned diplomat Bruce Laingen, was a literary coup.

But the Society also benefited from the rising tide that lifts all boats, for more and more people were being attracted to autograph collecting. Joseph Maddalena, a California dealer, estimated in 1990 that the total number of collectors was approaching 100,000. Although Charles Hamilton's auction gallery had disappeared in bankruptcy, a score of mail auctions had arisen in its place. "There's more depth to the market now," observed Marsha

Malinowski, a senior cataloguer at Sotheby's. "Before, you could count the heavy hitters on one hand."[2]

The lure of autographs was greater than ever, but the mores of collecting continued to change, and not necessarily for the better. The *Wall Street Journal* observed:

A new breed of document hounds, some with dollar signs in their eyes, is flooding the field once dominated by a small circle of scholars, dealers and private collectors. The demand has sent prices soaring.

Inevitably, the old guard is squaring off against the new. Old-line collectors say newcomers often treat pieces as high-yield investments rather than irreplaceable historical documents. They also warn that those jumping on the bandwagon for profit may get burned by the vagaries of speculation in the burgeoning market.[3]

In the late 1980s, the Manuscript Society, a bastion of the old guard, attempted to develop criteria for the catalogue descriptions of autographs. A committee chaired by Connecticut dealer Norman F. Boas drafted a pamphlet, *The Manuscript Society Criteria for Describing Manuscripts and Documents*, which, when published in 1990, attempted to impose a degree of order on cataloguing. Most important, it defined gradations in condition, such as the difference between a document that is *Fine* and one that is *Very Good*. In the years that followed, a number of established dealers chose to adopt the Society's criteria.

Since the Society's inception, its best-attended annual meetings had been those held in the country's main coastal cities. The Society is an international organization, however, and the success of the two London meetings lent encouragement to those on the board who favored an occasional gathering abroad.

Robert K. O'Neill of Boston College was the program chair in the early years of the 1990s. As curator of manuscripts at the John J. Burns Library, he had frequent professional contacts with his counterparts in Irish institutions, and he suggested Dublin as a promising site for an annual meeting. With the board's approval, O'Neill arranged a program that offered six days in the Irish Republic and two more in Northern Ireland.

In the end, 88 members attended at least part of the meeting in Ireland, which began with two days in Galway. There, members visited Coole Park, the site of the home of dramatist Lady Gregory and the location of a famous autograph tree where the carved initials include those of George Bernard Shaw, Sean O'Casey, and John Masefield. From there they visited Thoor Ballylee, the summer home of William Butler Yeats, where Yeats's son,

Michael, offered some charming recollections of growing up in the Tower. Back in Galway, Thomas Kenny, proprietor of a famous bookstore, led the group on a walking tour of the town.

The trip from Galway to Dublin was by way of Clonmacnois, a sixth-century monastery overlooking the Shannon River. Despite its repeated sacking by various invaders, Clonmacnois, with its round towers and Celtic crosses, remains the best-preserved early monastic site in Ireland.

In Dublin, Society members visited Trinity College, the National Library, and St. Patrick's Cathedral, where Jonathan Swift had served as dean. Other highlights included a tour of Dublin to examine the haunts of author James Joyce, and an evening at the Abbey Theatre, the national theater of Ireland, where members saw a modern version of O'Casey's *The Plough and the Stars*.

After four nights in Dublin, buses took some Society members to Belfast for a two-day postconference visit. Those who thought this portion of the trip would be an anticlimax were mistaken; many regarded their visits to the Giant's Causeway and to the University of Ulster's library to be among the highlights of the meeting.

A footnote to the annual meeting in Ireland: So far as is known, this is the only such meeting that has spawned a romance. Without much notice by anybody else two young people who attended with their parents—Mary Briggs, who was working in London as an editor, and Peter Price, an air traffic controller in California—struck up a friendship that ripened with correspondence and transatlantic visits and culminated in their marriage six months later.

The Society returned to the United Kingdom in 1996 for a nine-day visit to Scotland. John D. Haskell of the College of William and Mary, who had become program chairman two years earlier, organized a program that began with two days in Glasgow. There, visits to the Glasgow University Library and the adjacent Hunterian Museum (renowned for its outstanding Whistler Collection), the university archives with its brewing and shipbuilding records, the Glasgow Cathedral, and the famous Burrell Collection, thoroughly engaged the attendees.

A short bus trip to the east brought members to Edinburgh. There, a reception in the banking rooms of the 301-year-old Bank of Scotland, overlooking the Princes Street Gardens, included an exhibition of banking manuscripts. A morning at the National Library of Scotland, featuring an enthusiastic presentation by Iain G. Brown, was a high point of the meeting, as members were able to examine manuscripts of Sir Walter Scott and Adam Smith, among others.

A stop at St. Giles' Cathedral, where John Knox once served as minister, was followed by an afternoon at Edinburgh Castle, with its magnificent view all the way to the North Sea. A manuscript exhibition at the Edinburgh University Library, mounted epecially for the Society, included a fragment from an antiphoner from the 13th-century Inchcolm Abbey, the ruins of which Society members were able to visit that same afternoon.

Patrick Cadell, the Keeper of the Records of Scotland (the equivalent of our national archivist), welcomed the group to the conservation scripts, including three letters of George Washington, were on view. The meeting concluded with a gala banquet, in the Great Hall of the Royal College of Physicians of Edinburgh.

Thirty-eight Society members elected to stay two additional days for visits to Traquair House, the oldest continuously occupied house in Scotland; Dryburgh Abbey, the burial place of Scott; and Abbotsford, Scott's home in the Borders, where the visitors were welcomed by two of Scott's descendants. A tour of Glamis Castle, the ancestral home of the Queen Mother, lunch at the Old Course Hotel at St. Andrews, and a visit to Falkland Palace, the hunting residence of the Stuart monarchs, brought a splendid conclusion to the Society's fifth meeting outside the United States.

In February 1986, David Zullo, proprietor of a Gaithersburg, Maryland, bookshop, telephoned an occasional customer, William Turner, who was said to own some Virginia-related books and manuscripts that he was prepared to sell. Zullo, who had recently spoken with the head of the book department at theVirginia State Library, thought that the library might want to purchase Turner's material. Turner was interested in selling and consigned about 150 items to be sold on a commission basis. Zullo in turn forwarded them to the Virginia State Library for consideration.[4]

On February 27 a library staff member informed Zullo that 56 of the items consigned were being examined to determine whether they had ever been state property. The implication was that if they *had* once belonged to the state, Virginia planned to replevin them. Zullo was advised that he should address any questions to Dr. Louis Manarin, the state archivist. When Zullo told Turner what had happened, Turner called Arkansas dealer Gary Hendershott, to discuss his problem. Hendershott urged him to get in touch with Bart Cox, an expert in replevin law.

Cox recommended that Zullo demand return of the documents; he did so in a letter to Manarin dated March 3, 1986:

> If you felt inclined to pursue your action under the [replevin] law, you could have made xerox copies of the questionable material and returned the originals

to me. . . . To withhold this material as you now intend to do is an infringement upon my rights and upon the personal property of my client. Until it was proven beyond doubt that this material was not rightfully the owner's, your confiscation is an illegal act.

In replying to Zullo, Manarin returned eight items that he judged not to be public records, but ignored the substance of Zullo's protest. There the matter rested until April, when Manarin wrote to Zullo as follows:

We have completed our initial examination and study of the 48 items retained for that purpose.

As a result of our examination and study, we have grouped the items into three categories. . . . The items listed in Category 1 are Virginia public records which have strayed from public custody. Therefore, we are retaining them. We will pay a total care and keeping fee of $500 for all of these items. The items listed in Category 2 are very likely Virginia records, and because of their Virginia interest and connection we will purchase them for a total sum of $300. . . . The items listed in Category 3 are items that either are not, or do not appear to be, Virginia public records, and we are returning them herewith.

Turner was understandably furious. His first action was to tell all dealers with whom he dealt what had happened and to urge them to exercise great caution in dealing with institutional buyers in Virginia.[5] He concluded that the value of his documents did not justify going to court but wrote an article on his experience for *Antiquarian Bookman*, quoting Cox as saying that Manarin's action constituted an unjustified seizure of personal property.[6] He warned owners of Virginia documents to keep them in a safe place— "enjoy, study, fondle, etc., but under no circumstances let them become public knowledge."[7]

At the beginning of 1991, Jack D. Hamilton, proprietor of Hamilton's Rare Books in Williamsburg, Virginia, had never heard of Louis Manarin or David Zullo. Hamilton did far more business in books than in manuscripts. Nevertheless, in January 1991 he paid $2,000 to a local collector for a box of old Virginia documents that the collector had bought decades before in a Florida flea market. It was a mixed bag, including a 1687 inventory of Major Robert Beverly's worldly possessions, the 1698 will of one Mary Atwood, and papers relating to the emancipation of a slave girl, Daphne, in 1806.[8] It also included the charter of the town of Urbanna, in Middlesex County—a town near the mouth of the Rappahannock River best known for its oyster festival.

Hamilton had planned to offer his material to the Virginia Historical Society. Then, thinking of the Urbanna charter and of the fact that many of the documents related to Middlesex County, he showed them to his contacts at the Urbanna Public Library. The library staff were impressed with Hamilton's find and hopeful of acquiring the 81 Middlesex documents. Davidson J. Gill, a member of the board of supervisors, made an appointment with Hamilton to inspect the documents on February 11.

When Gill showed up at Hamilton's shop, he was accompanied by Bill Turner's nemesis, the state archivist, Louis Manarin. In the course of examining the documents, Manarin observed at one point that he could tell by the way that some were folded that they were public records. Manarin said that he would have to take the documents with him to determine their status, but that he could report back within 10 days. Hamilton did not care for this arrangement.

> Both men are wandering around my shop so I call them back together and tell them that it doesn't sound like a wise business decision to turn over items that I have bought in good faith. I have them in my possession and . . . they have shown me nothing to indicate that they have the right or authority to take them.[9]

Hamilton decided that his original inclination to offer the documents to the Virginia Historical Society may have been the correct one, and the following day he drove to Richmond. There he told a historical society representative, Lee Shepard, of his dealings with Gill and Manarin, but Shepard assured him that the historical society was still interested in purchasing the documents. On February 15 Hamilton called on Shepard again, and they agreed on a price of $40,000 for the Middlesex material.

A painful message awaited Hamilton at his shop, however. A letter from Supervisor Gill informed him that the state had filed a court order to seize the Middlesex documents. Hamilton telephoned Shepard, who told him that the historical society still wanted the documents if it could obtain clear title. But at that moment Hamilton's prospects appeared bleak.

A bit of background may be helpful here. The 1970s and 1980s were marked by an unusual phenomenon: "patrimony" laws enacted by various states and localities in an attempt to reclaim historic documents that had left their custody. Such laws, of course, followed decades in which government entities had discarded tons of deeds, land grants, and related correspondence. The common law doctrine of replevin was a handy weapon in the implementation of these patrimony laws.

In 1976 the state of Virginia had repealed an earlier replevin statute and replaced it with the Virginia Public Records Act (VPRA), which required that all papers determined to be "public records" were to be returned to the state. Nothing was said of seizure, but neither was anything said of compensation to the owner. So it was that on February 11, 1991, Middlesex County petitioned under the VPRA for the return of Hamilton's 81 documents. Four days later, officials of Isle of Wight County took similar action on 50 other documents that Hamilton had offered for sale, including slave records, deeds, and wills from the eighteenth century.[10]

On February 17, Circuit Judge William L. Person Jr. gave state archivist Louis Manarin 60 days to examine the Middlesex documents and scheduled a hearing for May 17. Hamilton had hired as his counsel a Newport News attorney, Rick Reiss, and Reiss's pretrial deposition of Manarin included the following exchange:

Q. Is the seizure of public records one of the functions of the Archives and Record Division [of the Virginia State Library and Archives]?

A. It is an activity that can be utilized to bring records under the jurisdiction of the Court so that it can be determined by the Court the true nature of these documents.

Q. If you were to list all of the responsibilities of the Archives and Records Division, would participation in the seizure of public records from private hands be listed?

A. It's one of the activities, yes.[11]

Meanwhile, Hamilton, like Bill Turner, had been advised to consult the Manuscript Society in the person of Bart Cox. Cox recommended to President Mary Schlosser that the Society support Hamilton with an amicus curiae brief, and Schlosser agreed. She also authorized a $1,000 direct contribution to Hamilton's defense fund. (Ultimately, the Society contributed more than $10,000 to the Hamilton defense.) The Society's brief, drafted by attorney Kathleen Taylor Sooy, included the following:

It is the position of the Manuscript Society that the [Virginia Public Records Act] as interpreted by the County offends both the United States and Virginia Constitutions. Only if the Act is interpreted by the Court to authorize the recapture of documents in which the County had a valid ownership interest under the common law and contemporaneous statutes can a taking of such documents without compensation be constitutional in this suit and others.

The County's interpretation of "public records" subject to seizure under the Act goes far beyond the traditional and common law understanding of what a public record is. The County's interpretation would sweep into the Act's fold documents that for centuries have been in private hands, paid for with private money and considered by law to be privately owned documents.[12]

Although the Society's brief focused on the constitutional issue, the court was actually being asked two questions: whether the seizure of privately held documents under the VPRA was constitutional, and whether Hamilton's 81 documents constituted "public records." Judge Person heard arguments on May 17, 1991, and delivered a mixed verdict on June 29.

First, the court rejected all arguments related to the constitutionality of the VPRA and the state's action in seizing Hamilton's material. It concluded that public records belong to the state and that there is no statute of limitations to bring suit for their return. Having dismissed the constitutional issue, Judge Person then held that although there was no evidence that Hamilton's documents had been improperly removed from government files, many qualified as "public records" under a common law definition. He then passed judgment on each of the papers in contention, determining that 38 of the 81 should go to the state, the remainder to Hamilton.

Clearly, Person had decided the case on the narrowest possible grounds. Nevertheless, Scott Petersen, a lawyer and Society member, writing in *Manuscripts*, saw the outcome as more favorable than it first appeared:

> For the first time, the State of Virginia has been challenged and lost. Louis Manarin will no longer be able to blithely appropriate the documents of private citizens which *he thinks* are public records, which he has been doing for 20 years. Citizens will become more defiant and will win. Incidentally, Louis Manarin is livid because for him this case is a loss. All of his testimony was rejected by the Judge. He has pleaded with the Virginia Attorney General to appeal the ruling. There will be no appeal.
>
> More importantly, the Court said that the Virginia Public Records Act cannot apply to records created before the adoption of the Act (1976). The only exception which allows the State to stake claims to privately-held material is if [a document] clearly falls within the old common law definition.[13]

Of all the replevin cases in which the Manuscript Society had played a part, it may have had its greatest influence in the Hamilton case. Although several organizations contributed to Hamilton's legal defense fund, the $10,000 provided by the Manuscript Society was by far the largest. Without the Society's backing, Hamilton told the *Norfolk Virginian-Pilot*, "I would have had to quit."[14]

The Hartranft Replevin Case

The name of General John Hartranft is not a household word, even in his native Pennsylvania, but he has a secure place among combat commanders of the Civil War. He led a regiment at the battles of Antietam and Second Manassas and was awarded the Medal of Honor for bravery. His most memorable brush with history, however, occurred after the fighting, when he was appointed provost marshal for Washington, D.C. As such, he was responsible for security in the nation's capital during the period of the trial and execution of John Wilkes Booth's fellow conspirators in the assassination of Lincoln.

In 1965, as the nation commemorated the centennial of the Civil War, General Hartranft's grandson, Hartranft Stockham, donated a portion of the general's papers to Gettysburg College. In addition, he placed on loan a larger group of more than 50 items, including letters exchanged at the time of the conspirators' trial between Hartranft and his military superior, General Winfield S. Hancock.

The correspondence between Stockham and Gettysburg College indicates clearly that the Lincoln-related material was only on loan. "It is my understanding," the president of Gettysburg College, C. A. Hanson, wrote to Stockham in 1965, "that the only papers that you wish returned are the documents and records on the prosecution of the Lincoln assassins but that you would wish to keep these on loan with us for several years." Later that year, Hanson wrote Stockham that the material on loan "will be properly released to you at any time should this be your wish."

Stockham died in 1983, with his papers still on loan to Gettysburg College. By this time the college had a new president, Gordon Haaland. In October 1993, Stockham's daughter, Helen Shireman, wrote to the college requesting the return of the material placed on loan nearly three decades earlier. The college failed to respond. Then, on January 18, 1994, President Haaland informed Mrs. Shireman: "We have performed an internal investigation concerning the Hartranft documents, and . . . it is our conclusion that the College is the sole owner of the General's papers."

When Gettysburg College clung to this position, Mrs. Shireman went to court. In the absence of any deed of gift in conflict with the earlier Stockham-Hanson correspondence, her legal position appeared to be a strong one. But when Gettysburg College realized that it was in danger of losing the documents, it sought to deny them to the Shiremans. It sent the disputed documents to the National Archives. The college announced that it was prepared to give up its claim to the Hartranft papers so long as the "military records" went to the federal government

But were the Hartranft papers "military records"? In part because the National Archives was not created until 1934, the government has a long history of claiming documents—now in private hands—that it maintains are government property. Few private owners of historical materials are in a position to take on the government in court, and the Shiremans were not among the few. Despite offers of assistance from the Manuscript Society and a number of Civil War buffs, the Shiremans felt obliged to give up title to the papers.

Scott Petersen, a Chicago attorney and Manuscript Society trustee, believes that the government goes after only small fry. Says Mr. Petersen: "I would venture to say that Harvard and Yale and institutions like the University of Virginia and the University of California all have warehouses of stuff that could be considered valuable federal records. Why not go after the big guys?"

—Adapted from an article by John M. Taylor in the
Wall Street Journal, June 6, 1995.

CHAPTER 17

Word Shadows of the Great

When Walt Whitman was seeking a clerkship in Washington during the Civil War, one of his assets was a letter of recommendation from the respected (and respectable) Ralph Waldo Emerson. Attempting to assist Whitman, a friend showed it to Secretary of the Treasury Salmon P. Chase. When Chase refused to help, because the poet's writings "have given him a bad repute," Whitman's friend reached to retrieve his letter. The secretary declined to give it up. "I have nothing of Emerson's in his handwriting," Chase remarked, "and I shall be glad to keep this."[1]

This anecdote is one more example of the pervasive appeal of an autograph. Most thoughtful people can appreciate a document that, at minimum, reflects a moment in the life of a celebrated figure and, at best, reflects that person's thought or an important moment in his or her career. Thus it is hardly surprising that the ranks of autograph collectors have included a number of persons who were notable in their own right, from Edgar Allan Poe and Jerome Kern to Franklin D. Roosevelt and Robert Kennedy. Indeed, Poe is said to have remarked, "Next to the person of a distinguished man, we desire to see his portrait; next to his portrait, his autograph."

Although professionals in the autograph world occasionally affect an air of déjà vu regarding run-of-the-mill autographs—Lincoln, after all, signed thousands of military commissions during the Civil War—unique items stir even the most blasé. When Stephen Massey, director of Christie's International Book Department, was asked which autographs had given him the greatest thrill, he replied, "I believe the original hand-drawn survey map of the Mason-Dixon line that I got from the Chew family of Philadelphia. Also, Einstein's letter to President Franklin Roosevelt urging him to start the Manhattan Project—a letter that ushered us into the nuclear age."[2]

People have come to collect autographs from many paths, and chance has often played a role in stimulating their interest. California collector Bill Coleman recalls how he made his first acquisition in 1952, when he visited an antiques fair. Hanging in the booth of one dealer was a badly framed document, the text in old type, that appeared to have been signed by George Washington. The dealer would not warrant the signature, but Coleman thought that for $50 he would take a chance. This serendipitous purchase— for the paper was the discharge of a Revolutionary soldier, authentically signed by Washington—launched Coleman on the collecting career that he is still pursuing more than four decades later.[3]

The Society's executive director, David Smith, began his career as a manuscript librarian while still a teenager, working as an assistant in the Huntington Library in San Marino, California. As a young man interested in history, he was fascinated to see that diligence could compensate to a degree for limited financial resources in assembling a collection. Smith decided to start a literary collection, beginning with Willard Huntington Wright, who wrote detective novels under the pseudonym S. S. Van Dine. Doing considerable detective work himself, Smith located the lawyer who had handled Wright's estate, who in turn referred him to Wright's former secretary. After a friendly exchange of correspondence, the secretary gave Smith a treasure trove of material still in her possession—letters, contracts, and manuscripts. Later, Smith also contacted relatives of the writer, who added to his collection. Today, David Smith's Van Dine collection is perhaps the finest in private hands.

One of the benefits that a Manuscript Society member derives from the annual meetings is the opportunity to exchange ideas with fellow collectors. Occasionally, however, discretion may be in order. David Coblentz, a onetime Society president, told of having come to know Dr. Otto Fischer of Detroit through the Society. One of Coblentz's primary collecting interests was the letters of General Nathanael Greene, and at one annual meeting he held forth at some length to Fischer on his fascination with the Revolutionary general. In the year that followed, Coblentz noticed that dealers who previously had routinely offered him Greene letters were no longer doing so. He found out that his friend Dr. Fischer had persuaded dealers to put him at the top of their lists for Greene material. Annoyed though he was, Coblentz retained a degree of friendship for Fischer. "He is a most fascinating fellow," Coblentz wrote to Herbert Klingelhofer, "and has told me lots of things about autographs that I would never have known otherwise."[4]

Autographs mean different things to different people. For all the satisfaction a collector may gain from the purchase of an important autograph, original documents become truly important when they shed new light on historic people or incidents. So it was with rare book dealers Leona Rostenberg and Madeleine Stern in 1942, when Rostenberg was assisting her partner in research for a new biography of Louisa May Alcott. They had just completed a useful interview with an Alcott collector, Carroll Atwood Wilson, when Wilson issued a challenge. "Miss Rostenberg," he remarked, "many of us are convinced that Louisa used a pseudonym to write sensational stories. You discover the pseudonym!" In Stern's recollection:

Leona found the answer in the manuscript room of Harvard's Houghton Library, where silence reigned supreme as the two of us plowed through masses of Alcott manuscripts, letters, family papers and memorabilia. Suddenly the silence was shattered by a warwhoop. Leona Rostenberg had found a clutch of five letters from a Boston publisher to "Dear Miss Alcott"—letters that would change forever the image of the Children's Friend.

The letters had been written in 1865 and 1866 by James R. Elliott of the Boston publishing firm Elliott, Thomes & Talbot. Thanks to these five letters we knew, in 1942, that Louisa May Alcott had taken the pseudonym A. M. Barnard to write thrillers for a periodical titled *Flag of Our Union*.[5]

The Rostenberg-Stern discoveries began a revolution in Alcott scholarship. Stern completed a critically acclaimed biography of Alcott and in 1975 edited a volume of four of Alcott's pseudonymous potboilers titled *Behind a Mask: The Unknown Thrillers of Louisa May Alcott*. The morning after its publication Stern was a guest on the *Today* show, and the hoopla began. Between 1975 and 1995 she edited four more volumes of Alcott's thrillers. Among the topics they dealt with were transvestitism, Hindu thuggism, hashish experimentation, and the power struggle between the sexes. "Never again," one reviewer wrote, "will you have quite the same image of this particular 'little woman.' "[6]

For dealers, autographs are a remunerative if highly competitive livelihood, enlivened by occasional moments of humor. Ken Rendell recalls how, in about 1986, he offered the late Malcolm Forbes the original manuscript of Julia Ward Howe's "Battle Hymn of the Republic" for $100,000. Forbes turned it down. Rendell then sold it to John W. Middendorf, who consigned it to Christie's a couple of years later. The purchaser there was Forbes, who paid $200,000—exactly twice the price at which Rendell had earlier offered it to him.[7]

Florida dealer Joseph Rubinfine first began dealing in autographs while raising chickens on the family dairy farm in New Jersey. In his recollection:

We hoped the phone would ring with an autograph order, and when it rang one day my wife Ruth was unprepared for a man who introduced himself as John Campbell and said he wanted to buy some pullets. "Pullets" can sound quite a bit like "poets," and Ruth didn't hear him exactly right. A quick lineup flashed through her mind: Frost and Field, Longfellow and Lowell, Shelley, Byron and Keats! "Anyone in particular?" she asked. A considerable pause followed, then Campbell said, "No, just any you want to get rid of. I had a small flock in California and I miss them."

Given this clue, Ruth was able to close on the sale of a dozen pullets, without having to explain what we now did for a living.[8]

Although it has never been necessary for one to be a millionaire to collect important autographs, money has always helped. David Karpeles, a California realtor, caught the bug in midlife, on a visit in 1978 to the Huntington Library in San Marino, California. There, he and his wife viewed the pass that President Lincoln had given one of his bodyguards on the night he was killed. "We asked some questions," Karpeles recalled, "and we found out that this little pass is nothing, that there are documents changing hands all the time that would make you faint."[9]

Karpeles decided to go into big-time collecting while important autographs were still available. Over the years he picked up outstanding items, including a proclamation by President Washington in 1789 establishing the first national Thanksgiving; the provisional constitution of the Confederate States of America, drafted by General Thomas Cobb of Georgia; and Richard Wagner's manuscript of the "Wedding March" from *Lohengrin*. "Finding a great document," Karpeles told one interviewer, "is better than cotton candy, watermelon, and sex."[10]

Unlike many collectors, Karpeles is more than willing to share his treasures, many of which are on display in five museums in various parts of the country. A highlight of the Manuscript Society's 1995 annual meeting in Seattle was a visit to the Karpeles exhibit hall in nearby Tacoma.

Stephen Bumball, a New Jersey business executive, was a special agent with U.S. Army Counterintelligence at the end of World War II. On April 30, 1945, his unit entered Munich and billeted in the home of a retired German general, Franz Ritter von Epp. The general was a collector, and he enjoyed showing Bumball his fine library, including the decoration King Ludwig III of Bavaria awarded him admitting him into the German nobility and allowing him to add the coveted *von* to his name. As Bumball recalled, "It was a most attractive document, and I sort of wished he would present it to me or that I could declare it *Beschlagnahmt*, that is, confiscated. Unfortunately, he did not present it to me, and I could not in good conscience confiscate it."

Decades later, after Bumball had built up a distinguished collection of World War II autographs, a friend told him about a German who had some

World War II material for sale. Among the documents was von Epp's Bavarian decoration, which Bumball was delighted to purchase some 42 years after he had first set eyes on it in war-ravaged Munich.[11]

The issue of material "liberated" from Germany at the end of World War II is pertinent in the world of autographs as in art. In 1945, a U.S. Army soldier, Cameron Anderson, found a fourteenth-century legal document near the Grossgrundlach Castle outside Nuremburg. He took it home and several decades later sent a copy to the Morgan Library, saying that he would like to return the document if it had appreciable value or significance. The library contacted the appropriate authorities in Germany, and in 1991 Anderson and his wife were invited to Germany for a ceremony in which they returned the document to Baron Helmut Haller von Hallenstein, whose family owned Grossgrundlach Castle.[12]

In contrast, the autographs of Hitler and his henchmen have inspired no such regard for history or respect for ownership. A considerable number of documents from the Third Reich—almost all removed from its ruins—continue to be traded in the United States and elsewhere without undue concern about the legal niceties.

The opportunities for specialization in autographs are perhaps less than in philately, but are still remarkable. H. Wesley Marans, a New England real estate developer, at one time had a collection of some 5,000 signed photographs. Among them were extraordinary rarities such as the nineteenth-century sharpshooter Annie Oakley and World War I flying ace Manfred von Richtofen.

Marans first became interested in the field when a friend bought a signed photograph of gangster Al Capone. Shortly thereafter, Marans happened to walk by Goodspeed's Book Shop in Boston, where he saw a number of signed photographs in the window. "They were $3 or $4 apiece, so I bought them," he recalls. Gradually, Marans came to regard signed photographs as something special. They reflected how the subjects viewed themselves.[13]

For all the highs produced by autograph finds, any collecting field includes disappointments as well. Richard Maass recalls how, in the 1950s, a fellow collector, Nat Stein, approached him with a proposition. Parke-Bernet Galleries was soon to auction one of several "souvenir" copies of the Gettysburg Address—copies penned by Lincoln for sale by charities. Stein thought that the New York Public Library should have a copy, and that a group of local collectors should be formed to buy the Parke-Bernet copy and then be reimbursed, in whole or in part, by voluntary contributions from the schoolchildren of the city.

Maass liked the suggestion, so he and Stein called on Arthur Swann, Parke-Bernet's vice president for books and autographs, to examine the document and to ask what price he expected it to realize. Swann replied that the Lincoln lot was the most important item of Americana to be offered for many years and that it would probably sell for more than $150,000. Maass and Stein left disappointed, convinced that such an amount was well beyond their reach.

They went to the sale anyhow. The sales room was packed and there was a ripple of muted conversation when the auctioneer reached the Gettysburg Address. Bidding began at $25,000 and progressed in $5,000 increments to $40,000, at which point there appeared to be only two bidders. At $50,000 the auctioneer could not get another $5,000 advance so he accepted one of $1,000. The lot was finally knocked down for $53,000.

Maass and Stein were both angry and astonished. Had they not been given such an exaggerated estimate, they might well have raised enough to purchase a fine Lincoln document for the New York Public Library. Instead, Maass learned, it had gone to a one-time Cuban ambassador to the United States who was not even an autograph collector.[14]

Auction sales are dramas, because of the intense competition they generate and because, as in most athletic competitions, there is only one winner. In the winter of 1988, Christie's put up for sale a portion of the famed Estelle Doheny collection, including a remarkable letter written by Caesar Rodney of Delaware, a Signer of the Declaration of Independence. There are precious few letters by any of the 56 Signers which were written on the critical date—July 4, 1776. Of these, only that by Rodney refers directly to the signing and its importance. Writing to his brother, Rodney told of his eleventh-hour arrival in Philadelphia for the signing:

I arrived in Congress (tho detained by thunder and Rain) time Enough to give my Voice in the matter of Independence. It is determined by the thirteen United Colonies with out even one decenting [sic] Colony. We have now got through with the Whole of the Declaration and ordered it to be printed so that you will soon have the pleasure of seeing it.

A delegation from Delaware attended the sale, determined to acquire this historic letter, which Christie's had estimated to sell at between $100,000 and $150,000. The Delaware Historical Society hoped to make the letter the crown jewel in its collection of Rodney family letters dating back to the seventeenth century and had received financial pledges from all over the state.

The bidding started at $50,000 and moved up quickly. At $350,000 the only remaining bidders were the Delaware Historical Society and a Bethesda, Maryland, construction executive, Albert Small. At $380,000 the

Delaware contingent dropped out of the bidding. For $400,000, plus a 10 percent commission, the letter went to Small, a collector who, outside the public eye, had gathered an outstanding collection of Signers, including a number of items dating from 1776. Small, noting the disappointment of many in attendance, quickly left the auction room to savor his triumph.[15]

In its fifth decade, the Society could look back with satisfaction on a successful publications program, the launching of the Manuscripts Database, and a series of informative and enjoyable annual meetings. But, as President Ellen Shaffer had remarked in 1967, for the Society to survive it must have something distinctive to offer. Alas, the continuing threats to private ownership of historic manuscripts served to provide the Society with what it had sometimes lacked: a mission. As one former president, Richard Maass, remarked in 1996:

The most valuable thing the Society can do is to push the position of private collectors against the government in replevin matters. I have felt since the Lewis and Clark case in the 1950s that the Society might as well go out of business if we don't fight replevin.[16]

At the November 1995 meeting of the Manuscript Society board, Bart Cox, who had closely followed the B. C. West and Hamilton replevin cases, addressed the board on the continuing replevin threat. Cox then made a dramatic offer: If the Society would raise $10,000 from its members for a replevin fund, he would make a matching grant of $10,000 in securities. After a brief discussion Cox's offer was gratefully accepted, and within a few months most of the $10,000 had been paid or subscribed.

Nonetheless, the board and the membership as a whole continue to hope for an accommodation among collectors, government bodies, and institutions. All are devoted to the concept of the preservation of the world's documentary heritage, and all are in a position to advance this objective. Fortunately for collectors everywhere, the Manuscript Society continues to uphold the rights of private collectors, as well as to promote the satisfactions that come from pursuing "word shadows of the great."

Presidents of the Manuscript Society

Joseph E. Fields, 1948–50

Richard M. Lederer, 1950–51

Justin G. Turner, 1951–53

Colton Storm, 1953–54

Richard Maass, 1954–56

Nathaniel E. Stein, 1956–58

Gordon T. Banks, 1958–60

David C. Mearns, 1960–62

David H. Coblentz, 1962–64

Stuart B. Schimmel, 1964–66

Ellen Shaffer, 1966–68

L. Quincy Mumford, 1968–70

Herbert E. Klingelhofer, 1970–72

Kenneth W. Rendell, 1972–74

Rodney Armstrong, 1974–76

P. William Filby, 1976–78

Barbara McCrimmon, 1978–80

John M. Taylor, 1980–82

Winston Broadfoot, 1982–84

George L. Vogt, 1984–86

William R. Coleman, 1986–88

Philip H. Jones, 1988–90

Mary C. Schlosser, 1990–92

Robert K. O'Neill, 1992–94

Chris Coover, 1994–96

John D. Haskell, 1996–98

*Manuscript Society Policy on Replevin**

The Manuscript Society, in encouraging and supporting the hobby of collecting historical autographs, manuscripts, and documents, recognizes and endorses the lawful and legitimate trade of buying and selling such material (including the right of collectors and dealers to buy and sell). Inherent in the Manuscript Society's encouragement and support of the hobby which forms the backbone of the organization is an opposition to and denunciation of any unlawful or unethical trade of historical autographs, manuscripts and documents. The Society condemns the unlawful or unauthorized taking or theft of autograph materials. The Society will always encourage the prompt and safe return of such material to the rightful owner(s).

In recent years the Manuscript Society has become aware of the occasional spurious or otherwise unfounded claims by state or local governments or by other claimants to materials which are in private hands. The basis for such claims is that the materials at one time were the property or *may* have been the property of the claimant. Based upon this theory of entitlement, the claimants have demanded and seized the materials—from collectors or private citizens—based on the doctrine of replevin (or under similar legal basis).

The Manuscript Society is aware that there may be materials which have unlawfully strayed from lawful owners to third parties and that such materials occasionally become the subject of efforts to recover them. In cases where recent theft or unlawful taking can be proved or demonstrated, the Manuscript Society will encourage and support the return of the materials to the lawful owner.

*Revised 1994.

Where, however, a claim to material is based upon conjured theories that do not allege, prove or demonstrate prior ownership or any subsequent unlawful taking, the Society will support the collector's right or the private citizen's right to keep and maintain such material when that person demonstrates lawful title. The Manuscript Society will judiciously consider supporting, with its corporate voice and with its corporate funds, the rights of the subsequent bona fide purchasers to keep such materials against unsubstantiated claims.

All decisions of financial or other involvement, however, will only be made after careful and objective investigation and evaluation. Support will be rendered only on a case-by-case basis after a full discussion and democratic action by the Board of Trustees of the Manuscript Society.

What Should I Do with My Collection?*

Joseph E. Fields

With apologies to Miguel Cervantes and the late Randolph Adams, "Naked we come into this world, and naked we go out of it." Much as we would like to do so, we cannot take our collections with us. Practically speaking, it would serve no purpose. Regardless of where we may land in the hereafter, there will be many opportunities for autograph collecting; great names abound on the far side of the River Styx and inside the Pearly Gates.

Every collector, no matter how modest, should come face to face with the question, "What shall I do with my collection?" May I urge you to give some thought to this problem while you are still among the living? Do not leave your decision to the courts. If you do make your own disposition, your estate will owe less in taxes. You yourself should have the say as to what is done with the collection.

A collector of autographs is fundamentally a sentimentalist. Without sentimentality no collector can be either successful or serious. Autograph collecting is a highly personal hobby; every item collected is unique. Nothing can bring you closer to the great figures of the past. You gain a knowledge of them that no other living person may have.

Let me illustrate with an anecdote from the lives of two or our great collectors of the past—Dr. Thomas Addis Emmet and Augustin Daly. In April 1889 Emmet was persuaded by Walter R. Benjamin to part with the great Lynch ALS which Benjamin then sold to Daly. Emmet was devastated by the loss of his prize item and subsequently appealed to Daly, as a matter of sentiment, to allow him to purchase it back, directly. With great magna-

*A panel discussion originally published in *Manuscripts* in 1953.

nimity Daly allowed Emmet to purchase the letter back for $3,250, plus a cut Lynch signature, a Thomas Heyward DS, and a Hancock ALS. Within eight days, seven letters passed between the two men. Their letters indicate that these men who lived in the same city never met personally.

One does not need to have a Lynch ALS in order to feel as the good doctor did. All collectors feel as he did about their collections. If you doubt it, try to pry even a trivial item away from a collector. Autograph collectors, being sentimentalists, are more than cognizant of the dilemma of disposing of their collections.

You have four choices if you are trying to decide what to do with your collection. First, you may give it to an heir, or to any other individual, during your lifetime. Second, you may will it to an heir on your death. Third, you may present it to an institution. Fourth, you may sell it privately or at public auction.

Let us take up each of these choices in somewhat more detail.

A GIFT DURING YOUR LIFETIME

Since 1976, U.S. law has permitted you to give up to $10,000 in one year to an individual without having to fill out any gift tax forms. The gross amount not subject to gift tax in 1983 was $275,000, rising in annual increments to a total of $600,000 in 1986 and thereafter.

WILL TO AN HEIR

If a collector has a legal heir who appreciates his collection, who will add to it, and who will make use of it, then the collector has a moral duty to dispose of it in this fashion. Unfortunately, all too seldom do we find the offspring of collectors sufficiently interested to be entrusted with the care, nurture, use, or disposal of an autograph collection. Before you will your collection to an heir, ask yourself whether the recipient is worthy of it. Will he use it? Does he appreciate its intrinsic and monetary value? Will he care for it properly? Only after carefully weighing these factors can you possibly make this decision. I speak from experience when I say there is nothing that gladdens the heart of a collector more than to pass on his collection to a son or daughter who will continue to use it, enlarge it, and give it the loving care it deserves.

PRESENT TO AN INSTITUTION

In the absence of an appropriate individual recipient, you may decide to present your collection to one of the many institutional depositories. This is more likely to be the preferred choice if your estate is so sizable that it would be advantageous to so dispose of it as a means of decreasing inheritance taxes. Giving a collection to an institution is not to be taken lightly. It requires more study and investigation than the two choices already discussed.

If you are thinking of presenting your collection to an institution you should consider these questions:

1. Is the institution capable of caring for your collection? Does it have the physical and custodial facilities to care for it or is it like the well-known New England historical society that has the papers of one of the prominent Revolutionary War generals stuffed into twelve large cardboard cartons in a completely helter-skelter fashion—all because there is no one available to arrange, catalogue, and index the material?

2. Will the institution make appropriate use of your collection? Will the material be made available for study by students? Will it be put on exhibit regularly and in an accessible place so that the public may view it conveniently? (May I draw this to the attention of the federal government, which has seen fit to deposit our three great state documents in the National Archives? A more difficult, inaccessible, and inconvenient place could not be found if they had tried.) Or will the institution do as 98 percent of the institutions have done—entomb the collection on its shelves and there let it remain unused, unpublished, unindexed, and unavailable?

3. Will your collection be appreciated? Will you and your gift soon be forgotten? The ivy climbs thick over the name of Wiebold at the University of Chicago, and the pigeons roost comfortably and serenely on the statue of James Buchanan Duke. Will you receive public recognition for your generosity or will you merely receive a short typed letter signed by the librarian, accepting your gift? Recently one of the large New England universities received from an alumnus a handsome gift consisting of numerous fine examples of first editions by an American author. All were desirable rarities. To this day the donor has received no recognition in the annual report of the library, while lesser contributors with more famous Back Bay names have received mention. Needless to say, the university probably will not receive the remainder of the extensive collection.

4. Will your gift serve the best interests of collecting, from the standpoint of both the private as well as the institutional collector? Cooperation between collectors and institutions is not a one-way street. The cooperation should flow freely in both directions. There has been an uninterrupted flow of autographic material into the files and shelves of institutions. This should not and must not be. There is no more certain way of sounding the death knell of collecting than by forever incarcerating autograph items in an

institution. It was private enterprise, manifested by such early collectors as Sprague, Tefft, Emmet, Gilmore, Gratz, and Dreer, that focused the attention of others onto the delights and pleasures of collecting. The result of the precedent and the course they set has been that for the past century most of the historical societies and similar public institutions have been conceived and perpetuated at the hands of collectors. Few of our great libraries and societies would exist today without the private interest manifested by collectors and their pursuits. Without such men as Morgan, Brown, Huntington, Folger, Clements, and many others, of what would our institutions consist? The custodians would have nothing to "custode." Probably there would not even be custodians. The private interest and rugged individualism of the collectors have served the institutions well.

THE CONSEQUENCES OF INSTITUTIONALIZATION

What will be the result if the steady procession of material into institutions continues and the source becomes dry? The desire to collect will be destroyed. There are evidences of atrophy setting in today. Without the incentive to collect, values will decline rapidly. The already groaning shelves of the institutions will be weighed down with paper in a mess so chaotic that it will defy all human efforts to untangle it. No institutional budget could withstand the strain of hiring the experienced help necessary to catalogue, transcribe, index, and file the material. I can name today a large number of institutions, including state and national archives, in that very predicament. If the trend continues, we may well be in the process of killing the goose that laid the golden egg.

Is planned destruction of material by institutions the answer to the problem? Who among us would be willing to decide whether a letter or document should be destroyed? If it is a matter of limited housing, restricted funds for hiring proper personnel, or shortage of time, then surely there are other more practical, economical, and moral solutions than destruction.

SOME SOLUTIONS

I would like to suggest that institutions sell duplicate and unwanted items. This would serve the public as well as the private interest. Certainly these items will bring more revenue at public or private sales than as scrap paper. In addition, they would provide abundant material to promote the private interest and perpetuate the system. Serving the private interest will more than repay the institutions by a greater enthusiasm and better support for their program. Their membership will increase—not with dead freight but with good, lively, and working members who will be a credit to the organization and have a genuine interest above and beyond merely participating as a civic duty.

Many institutions are hamstrung by legal restrictions imposed upon them by donors who forbid them to dispose of the gifts through sale or to trade them for other more desirable items. Some are even forbidden by the terms of the gift to allow removal of items from the library for purposes of exhibition. Do not shackle an institution with such provisos. Fields of interest change with time. What may be desirable today may in the future be of secondary interest and better sold or traded so that another more desirable item may be acquired. Make your gift with but one restriction— that the institution forever have its red carpet out to all deserving collectors and students, to anyone who is interested enough to stop, look, and listen. Permit the sale of your gift if it best serves the interest of the institution. Let the ultimate decision rest with the director. This implies faith in the management that your best intentions are carried out. The following deed of gift ensures that the spirit of your gift will be honored:

I, _____ , hereby give to the trustees of the University of _____ , for the use and benefit of the library, (here follows a description of the property). The said gift is to be without any conditions whatsoever and the donee shall have absolute discretion to retain the property herewith conveyed or to sell or to exchange the same or to make such other disposition of said property that shall seem wise and prudent to the director of the said library.

I should like also to advocate the appointment of collectors to the governing boards of institutions and libraries. Not many have, at the present time, done this. Collectors will help ensure the continuance of the best interests of collecting, private as well as institutional. They would be invaluable assets to the libraries they serve, for they have valuable insights into the problems of purchase, acquisition, rarity, value, authentication, and desirability, and other problems common to private as well as institutional collectors. The institutions have long wooed collectors as benefactors. Very few have thought well enough of them to place them at or near the helm.

SALE OR AUCTION

Assuming you have no suitable heir and there is no institution meeting the requirements you have established, then there is but one other course open to you—to sell your collection privately or at public sale. At least you may then be assured of several facts:

- The new owner will give the document loving care.
- The item will be appreciated.
- The item's sentimental value will be greater to the private collector than to the institutional collector.
- You will pass along to a fellow collector the pleasure you once enjoyed.
- You will have the personal satisfaction of placing your autographs on the public market where they may continue in the realm of public interest rather than being forever removed from a competitive market.
- By promoting a continuing interest in others you will bring about competition and thereby increase the value of autographs.
- You will have the personal satisfaction of dispersing material that will spread the word of our American heritage.

Perhaps all this has been best put by the familiar quotation from the will of the great French collector, Edmond de Goncourt:

My wish is that my drawings, my prints, my Curiosities, my Books—in a word, these things of art which have been the joy of my life—shall not be consigned to the cold tomb of a museum, and subjected to the stupid glance of the careless passer-by; but I require that they shall be dispersed under the hammer of the Auctioneer, so that the pleasure which the acquiring of each one of them has given me shall be given again, in each case, to some inheritor of my own tastes.

*   *   *   *   *

Robert F. Metzdorf

There are too many factors involved for anyone to give a categorical answer to an inquiry about what to do with an autograph collection. Some collections, by their nature, might well be destroyed when the collector is finished with them; others should be preserved at all costs. Some should be broken up and redistributed; still others should remain intact. The collector himself is faced with these and with many other problems, depending upon the nature of the collection under consideration, his own financial situation and the tax laws at the time of decision, his family obligations, his preferences, and even his prejudices. Collecting, to my way of thinking (and I became a collector before I became a curator), is one of the last strongholds of individual enterprise: you can collect whatever you choose, and nobody can tell you what you have to do with the things later on.

What are some of the considerations you should bear in mind when you are attempting to decide for yourself? Perhaps the only bit of advice that holds true for all cases is this: decide carefully, coolly, logically, and unemotionally after studying the collection, considering possible destinations for it, and securing the best advice available.

EN BLOC OR PIECEMEAL DISPOSITION?

Let us assume that you are about to make your will, or that for some reason you wish to dispose of the collection during your lifetime. If the reasons for the latter course are financial, you will wish to realize all you can from the material by selling it. The question immediately arises whether to sell en bloc or piece by piece. In selling a collection as a unit, you may sell it to a dealer, who will propose either to remarket it as a unit, thus preserving the identity of the collection (at least for a time), or to break it up and sell the contents individually. You may sell the material to an institution with the understanding that the autographs will be kept together as a unit (in which case you might have to shade the price a bit); or the institution may separate the items, intercollating some with its own holdings and selling other items.

Or you may sell the collection piecemeal. It may be put up at auction, with the more important items offered separately and the less important items grouped in lots. This has often been done, and I do not think the auction business is about to give up the ghost, so far as manuscripts are concerned, for want of suitable material to offer for sale.

Collectors feed principally on the products of attics and storage files. If the great and sometimes greedy institutions of our country seem to swallow up the entire available supply of one type of material, you may be sure that the collecting instinct is so strong, interest in the past so intense, and respect for the memory of the great so well founded that collectors will find new fields in which to satisfy the collecting urge, as well as the competitive instinct. The history of collecting proves it, as does the history of trade. I cannot tell you, of course, exactly what the new fields will be, but there are indications of some new directions that collecting will take. One such field is business and labor documents.

Another way of disposing of items one by one is to sell them to dealers or to other collectors. But bear in mind that, once the gems of a collection are gone, the remainder may be difficult to market.

The decision in selling a collection, no matter what method is used, should be based on the purpose the collector originally had in mind and on the financial situation of the vendor. Cost of acquisition as well as cost of dispersal should be considered, as should special tax situations that may exist at any given time and location. The advantages that can accrue through careful study of the tax laws and one's own financial position are many and varied, and no one should overlook them. If you are going to have an auction, get the soundest and coolest advice you can about the probable total of the sale; then figure the deductions of auction expense, and decide what to do.

You might go to a friendly librarian who is experienced in such matters, or you might very well go to a dealer. Happy are collectors who have dealer friends with whom they can talk over such problems! And happy are the dealers with collecting friends who bring such problems to them!

If the decision is favorable to continue with the plan, secure a favorable date for the sale, and do not accept a sale date without studying the other offerings of the season (in other auction rooms as well as the one you propose to use), competing public events, and any other factors that may apply. Instruct your executors to do all these things, if you do not plan to be around when the decisions are made. And be sure you have a clear title to all goods that you offer!

THE GIFT

If you are considering disposal by gift, there are other questions you should put to yourself. If you cannot come up with the answers, you should seek some trustworthy advice.

Where will the material be of most use to the public, and to that specialized branch of the public called scholars? Where will the manuscripts get the best care; that is, where will you find trained personnel, proper storage conditions, and good exhibition facilities? Will the new owner add material to the collection, and will the collection take on new life, instead of remaining static? Is there material already in the depository that will dovetail with your gift, making each of greater usefulness and interest? If the gift is made in your lifetime, will you be able to see it from time to time, work (or play) with it, add to it, and be sure it is getting proper care?

That is a fairly long series of questions. But the question method does underline one of my main points: nobody can tell you what to do with your collection, and no one should try to do so. My own opinion is that, if you have been smart enough to conjure up the idea of a significant collection of manuscript material, enterprising enough to secure the money to realize your ideal, diligent enough to learn the necessary background material, thoughtful enough to care for the collection properly, and clever enough to compete with others operating in the same field, then you are presumably perfectly capable of studying the situation and deciding what you want to do with your own collection.

Let us imagine that you have decided to give away your collection, either directly or by bequest, and that you have a preference about where it should go. You may favor a local historical society, a hometown library, your alma mater, a great library of national reputation, a particular institution that already possesses supplementary material (which means the things you wish you had in your own collection!), or a neighboring institution with which you have friendly relations. My advice would be that you talk over the matter with the librarian of whatever place you have in mind. Take along an inventory.

Then sit back and listen. You may be surprised. Not all librarians are insatiable octopuses, snaking in with greedy arms everything they can encompass. In fact, beware of such librarians, for their libraries may be storage places, historico-literary graveyards, not libraries for use. If you canvass your own experience, I think you will agree that most librarians are honest people, specialists who work for a living at their specialties, interested in historical and literary materials and concerned about the fate of them more than they are with their own prestige or any fleeting monetary rewards that acquisitiveness may bring them.

Your particular librarian may be very frank and tell you that he appreciates your offer, but that he cannot accept it—and he will be very sure to tell you why. He may not be able to meet your conditions, for example. If you wanted a separate room for the collection, and he does not have the space or does not agree that your collection deserves such a monument, he will have to say no. If the acceptance of the collection means taking on financial burdens that the library cannot assume—such as additional storage facilities, additional staff positions, or expensive reorganization—he will have to refuse.

In such a situation, if your mind is made up, you will have to refuse. In such a situation, if your mind is made up, you will need to consider "buying your way in," literally, as others have occasionally done, figuring out a cash gift or an endowment fund to supplement the donation of material, or otherwise overcoming obstacles. It is not always so easy to give something away as many people assume! There are, of course, many collections that any administrator in the country would give his eyeteeth to secure. But we are for the most part considering the average collection—if such a thing exists.

On the other hand, your adviser may tell you that your collection obviously belongs somewhere else. It may supplement an existing concentration of papers elsewhere, and should join it to complete a group that should never have been separated. Let me make a plea for the collections that should never be broken up—either by sale, gift, or sheer inadvertence. The advantages of having a person's papers in one place, for example, are too many to list: those who have worked with Emerson material at Harvard, the Boswell papers at Yale, or the William Henry Seward collection at Rochester (to mention but three that I have myself used) can testify to the truth of this. One of the great tragedies in this field in recent times was the sale some years ago of Sir Isaac Newton's papers, which are now scattered over several continents and can never be studied in one place.

Putting my advice into a slogan, I would say, "Discuss before you disperse, study before you select, and think before you get thanked."

* * * * *

Thomas R. Adams

Joseph Fields and Robert Metzdorf have thoroughly covered the various problems of what to do with one's collection. I completely agree with most of what they have said. As a commentator, therefore, I am reduced to picking but a single point from Dr. Fields's remarks on which I find I disagree with him. He objects to the steady flow of materials onto the shelves of institutions. He sees in this a drying up of the sources for autograph collectors, a destruction of the whole race of men like the Morgans, Browns, and Huntingtons, and, in general, "sounding the death knell of collecting."

If I may say so, this sounds very much like the group of booksellers who, in this century, have bemoaned the drying up of Americana as a field of collecting, as the Columbus letters and Bay Psalm Books have disappeared into institutions. Yet right under the very noses of these men the Edward Eberstadts and John Kohns have, with their customers, discovered a whole new field of collecting in western Americana and American literature.

Autographs, like books, have the capacity to grow both in number and in collectibility as the years go by. Collectors have always been in the vanguard of scholarship by searching out new fields to collect and providing the raw materials for new and enlarged study and understanding of our history. Just as the work of Peter Force was invaluable in creating collections for research in early United States history, so we shall always be deeply indebted to William Robinson Coe for his great collection of contemporary journals describing the opening of the American West.

The areas of human activity are so wide that all the archives and libraries in the country could not begin to cover them all by their own collecting. The recent growth of social, economic, and local history has opened vast new areas in which the historian badly needs the help of the collector. This, of course, is to say nothing of the whole field of literary scholarship.

The items one collector will cast aside in contempt another collector will eagerly seize upon. It is said that Wisdom, in assembling his collection on Thomas Wolfe, took every scrap of paper that might have some bearing on that author. And I am sure that he included things which many self-respecting autograph collectors would discard as unworthy. Yet the result is that today at Harvard there is the core from which most work on Wolfe must begin.

We all know that behind every great library from the Vatican to the Huntington lie many stories of the energy and devotion of collectors. The library is the product of the collector, and the institution serves him by providing a place in which his work will be preserved. Our institutions are not perfect, and they do not always carry out their functions properly. I hold no brief for the New England historical society that has allowed the papers of the Revolutionary War general to remain unsorted in cardboard boxes, but I would like to point out that at least they are there! There are many stories of important finds in overcrowded and understaffed libraries and archives. Had these same papers been in attics or barns, the chances are good that they would long since have been lost as wastepaper.

I recently found in the University of Pennsylvania Library a bound volume of manuscripts that contained President Monroe's veto of the Cumberland Road Bill. We know that it was given to us by Bloomfield H. Moore, a Philadelphia merchant of the 1870s, but we cannot discover how he got it. The federal government was notorious for the mishandling of its public papers during the nineteenth century. This major document of Monroe's presidency might well have been carted away by the trashman had it not been for a collector who saw its importance and the library that, despite its failure to recognize it for what it was, at least kept it from harm.

I fully agree with Dr. Fields that cooperation between institutions and collectors is not a one-way street. When the collector gives the results of his time, money, and knowledge to an institution, he should receive in return the assurance that his work will continue to live after him in the hands of scholars and to grow in the hands of the librarians. The institution should encourage and cooperate with the collector, not by providing him with things to collect, but by providing him with a background against which his collection will have some measure of security and stability in this troubled world.

*   *   *   *   *

Forest H. Sweet

"What shall I do with my collection?" This question is often asked of a dealer.

Dr. Fields is a collector. Mr. Metzdorf was a collector. Mr. Adams is the son of Randolph Adams, who, though he posed as a librarian, was the greatest collector I have known—and his son Tom was brought up on a collector's diet.

But there is another type of librarian, the so-called professional librarian, trained in a library science school and decorated with a bachelor's, master's, or doctor's degree in the mechanics of handling vast quantities of movable objects (books and manuscripts) and in the use of indexes, card catalogues, bibliographies, and other tools of the trade.

Librarians are schooled in making these tools and in administering their use by other employees. But a review of the curriculums of the various library schools shows no courses designed to give these students any knowledge of, or sympathy for, the collector's viewpoint. Graduates have proudly proclaimed to me, when I have asked whether they had any philosophical or sentimental or inspirational instruction, that theirs is a science, an exact body of knowledge.

Probably this kind of training is altogether fitting for work in a public library, a business or industrial library, the average state library, and some parts, at least, of university libraries, where the work is largely the mechanics of moving books from shelf to reader and back to shelf with a minimum of time and effort and expense, and where administration is devoted largely to keeping the employees reasonably happy on inadequate salaries, trying to have the books on the shelves ahead of the demand for them, and giving acceptable alibis when they are not. General Motors finds similarly "scientific" training advantageous to the nimble-footed young gentlemen who scurry about amongst the bins and shelves of the parts department to gather up the pieces necessary to put your car back into operating condition after you have wrapped it around a tree or worn it out by inadequate lubrication. They, too, have the indexes, the catalogues, the numbers, and other finding aids.

But while General Motors does not let these men design your car, similarly trained library technicians are sometimes put in control of fine collections. It happens easily. The president of the university is chosen because he is a good administrator and businessman. The library schools have to find jobs for their graduates, especially their Ph.D.'s. A Ph.D. is supposed to know everything, especially in university circles. The library job is open, a Ph.D. is out of work, the president is busy with ninety-seven other problems—so the appointment is made and that is one problem off the president's mind. What happens when library science, or any other science, is applied to your collection?

You can restrict the gift of your collection so that it must be kept, but you cannot restrict the gift so that it will be appreciated, used, sympathetically cared for, and enlarged by additions.

I have two suggestions to collectors asking what to do with their collections:

1. If you insist on giving your collection to an institution, buy a set of false whiskers and a wig and investigate the library or libraries you have in mind. Find out how they operate, what they have done with other collections that have been given them. Inquire into all their gift collections, not just one or two. If you are too busy to do that, hire spies to investigate and report to you.

2. Sell your collection for the highest price obtainable. If it ought to be kept together, the highest price should come from the library best equipped to make proper use of it. Appreciation is best expressed in a treasurer's check. The library worthy of having the collection can raise the money for what it really wants. Human nature being what it is, we all appreciate anything in direct ratio to the amount of effort necessary to get it.

Then, later, if you want a tax deduction as a benefactor of a learned institution, give them back the purchase money, with additions if possible, to carry on the collection and to prolong and extend its usefulness.

Did you ever see a dearly bought collection in cold storage?

*   *   *   *   *

Cecil K. Byrd

Mr. Sweet employs in his remarks a cliché that has become synonymous with laughter in American folklore: the librarian as a well-meaning, slightly addle-brained do-gooder. But there is some progress; he gives the present-day librarian a new personality. Today the professional librarians are pictured as officious busybodies hurtling their way through libraries, filled with misinformation, destroying in their feverish activities the precious heritage of our past as represented in books and manuscripts. Were it not that I know Mr. Sweet to be something of a humorist and that there may be more than a grain of truth in his remarks, I would be more heated in my rebuttal of his accusations.

Mr. Sweet accuses library-science-school–trained librarians of not being prepared emotionally, philosophically, historically, or esthetically to care for and administer collections of books and manuscripts. Trained on a diet of managerial science, they are equipped only to page and shelve books. The library schools have nothing in their programs designed to give the students an appreciation for the collector's viewpoint.

I do not know what Mr. Sweet means by "the collector's viewpoint." To me, a person who has a knowledge and appreciation of the origins of writing, and the historical development of the book in manuscript and printed form, and who realizes that many of our great libraries of today started with the books of a great collector, must, in some degree, have the collector's viewpoint. Each year at Indiana University I have an eager group of graduate students working for library science degrees who meet with me in the library twice each week for a course labeled, for want of a better name, "History of Books and Libraries." In this course we study human records from the primitive to the refined form, the manuscript and printed book in physical and spiritual aspects, and the great collectors and collections of the past and our own age. Surely this is proper background to make the professional librarian appreciate the private collector and his collection. Most other library schools offer similar courses.

There is a most important trend in professional library management that, if it continues, will lead to greater cooperation and mutual understanding between the librarian and the collector. I refer to the growing practice in many libraries of employing staff with a minimum of professional library school training and a maximum of subject background in English and American literature, history, economics, and other related subjects. Perhaps these subject specialists who have fed but lightly on the library-school curriculum can properly administer and nurture this hypothetical collection under discussion, even to Mr. Sweet's satisfaction.

Mr. Sweet has suggested that some collections that have been given to libraries have been placed in cold storage, where they languish, unloved and neglected. We all know of collections so treated. In some instances a collection receives this treatment because the collector is grievously at fault in the selection of a final repository for his collection. If an institution is known to have any interest in the subject represented by your collection and has given evidence of that interest by employing a staff who teach and do research in the area, the chances are good that your collection will not be given the cold-storage treatment. You are inviting the neglect of your collection by giving it to an institution that has never shown any curricular interest in your subject.

Actually, the problem of what to do with your collection is not a difficult one. If you can afford to give it away, there are enough libraries in this country who have demonstrated their ability to house, administer, and use every conceivable kind of rare book and manuscript collection. If you cannot afford to give it away, there are numerous competent, informed dealers from coast to coast who can advise you on marketing your materials.

Notes

CHAPTER ONE. A Meeting in Chicago

1. *New York Sun*, March 19, 1948.
2. Herbert Klingelhofer to the author, March 12, 1995.
3. Forest H. Sweet to Joseph Fields [Oct. 1947].
4. Forest H. Sweet to Joseph Fields, Jan. 12, 1960.
5. *Antiquarian Bookman*, May 29, 1948: 919.
6. John M. Taylor, "What's in a Name?" *Aloft*, Nov.-Dec. 1979.
7. Edmund Berkeley, ed., *Autographs and Manuscripts* (New York: Charles Schribner's, 1978), 46.
8. Quoted in Nicholas A. Basbanes, *A Gentle Madness* (New York: Henry Holt, 1995), 176.
9. Walter N. Eastburn, "The First Ten Years," 1.
10. Form letter [1948], Joseph Fields to "Dear Fellow Collector."
11. Allyn Ford to Charles Sessler, Dec. 23, 1947.
12. Richard Lederer to Justin Turner, April 20, 1948.
13. Mary Benjamin to Joseph Fields, Jan. 19, 1948.
14. Allyn Ford to Joseph Fields, Feb. 19, 1948.
15. Sol Malkin to Forest Sweet, March 5, 1948.
16. Mary Benjamin and others to Joseph Fields, March 5, 1948.
17. Gordon Banks to Joseph Fields, Feb. 26, 1948.
18. Joseph Fields to Mary Benjamin, March 21, 1948.
19. Mary Benjamin to Joseph Fields, April 2, 1948.
20. *New York Herald Tribune*, May 2, 1948.
21. University of Michigan News Service, May 18, 1948.
22. Joseph Fields, "Founding of the NSAC," *Antiquarian Bookman*, May 29, 1948.

CHAPTER TWO. Ford's Theatre and Other Capers

1. Forest Sweet to Joseph Fields, Feb. 27, 1956.

2. Leona Rostenberg and Madeleine B. Stern, *Old and Rare* (Santa Monica, Calif.: Modoc Press, 1988), 63–64.

3. Si Kahn, *Organizing* (New York: McGraw-Hill, 1982), 69.

4. NSAC Constitution, 1950.

5. Joseph Fields, "NSAC: Past and Future," *Antiquarian Bookman*, April 9, 1949.

6. Richard Lederer to Joseph Fields, April 12, 1948.

7. *New York World Telegram and Sun*, Dec. 8, 1950.

8. Allyn Ford to Joseph Fields, Feb. 14, 1948.

9. *Antiquarian Bookman*, April 9, 1949.

10. L. H. Butterfield, "For the Definitive Papers," *Autograph Collectors' Journal*, April 1949.

11. David C. Mearns, "Morsels of History," *Autograph Collectors' Journal*, April 1949.

12. *Autograph Collectors' Journal*, Oct. 1948, 23.

13. Merrill D. Peterson, *Lincoln in American Memory* (New York: Oxford University Press, 1994), 338.

14. *Washington Evening Star*, May 3, 1930.

15. Alexander Armour to Joseph Fields, Jan. 14, 1950.

16. *Library of Congress Bulletin*, vol. IX, no. 19: 4.

17. *Louisville Courier-Journal*, May 13, 1951.

CHAPTER THREE. "History in Your Hand"

1. *UCLA Librarian*, Nov. 16, 1956.

2. *Autograph Collectors' Journal*, Spring 1952: 58–59.

3. Charles Hamilton, *Auction Madness* (New York: Everest House, 1981), 76–78.

4. David C. Mearns to Colton Storm, Feb. 26, 1954.

5. *Christian Science Monitor*, May 15, 1952.

6. Undated [1952] press clipping.

7. Fields-Maass Oral History, August 1994, Reel 3.

8. *Washington Evening Star*, May 3, 1950.

9. Minutes, Board of Directors' meeting, May 5, 1952.

10. David Mearns to Gordon Banks, May 12, 1952.

11. *Autograph Collectors' Journal*, Summer 1952: 37.

12. Ibid., Fall 1952: 55.

13. Walter Eastburn to Justin Turner, July 14, 1952.

14. A transcript of this interesting discussion is found in the Society's anthology, Priscilla S. Taylor, ed., *Manuscripts: The First Twenty Years* (Westport, Conn.: Greenwood Press, 1984), and is included here as Appendix C.

15. Treasurer's Report, May 1, 1953–April 30, 1954.

16. *Autograph Collectors' Journal*, Winter 1953.

17. Report of Meetings, Los Angeles Chapter, April 28, 1952.

18. Report of the New York Chapter, April 23, 1953.

CHAPTER FOUR. David and Goliath: The Lewis and Clark Case

1. *Minneapolis Star*, undated clipping [1955].
2. Robert H. Bahmer, statement to the Society of American Archivists, Oct. 11, 1955.
3. Forest H. Sweet, "The Function of the Dealer in Relations to the Collection and Preservation of Historical Materials," address before the Society of American Archivists, Nov. 16, 1943.
4. Robert Metzdorf to Richard Maass, March 16, 1955.
5. *New York Times*, May 29, 1955.
6. Lyman Butterfield to Richard Maass, Nov. 21, 1955.
7. *Manuscripts*, Summer 1955: 214–15.
8. Justin Turner to Robert Metzdorf, June 23, 1955.
9. Justin Turner to Forest Sweet, June 4, 1957.
10. *Manuscripts*, Winter 1957. This issue contains the full text of Judge Nordbye's opinion.
11. Ibid., 6.
12. Louis Starr to Gordon Banks, July 1958.
13. Richard Maass, "President's Page," *Manuscripts*, Winter 1956.
14. Robert Metzdorf to Walter Eastburn, Nov. 6, 1956.
15. Donald F. Hyde to Richard Maass, Oct. 19, 1956.
16. Justin Turner to Donald Hyde, Oct. 18, 1956.

CHAPTER FIVE. Growing Pains

1. *Northwestern Library News*, May 4, 1956.
2. David Coblentz to Herbert Klingelhofer, Oct. 12, 1958.
3. Undated [1954?] memo from Richard Maass to the Publications Committee.
4. Justin Turner to Nat Stein, June 19, 1957.
5. Minutes, Board of Directors' meeting, Nov. 9, 1957.
6. Clyde C. Walton to Robert Downs, Aug. 28, 1958.
7. Unsigned "Memo for G.T.B. [Gordon Banks]," [1958].
8. Forest Sweet to Joseph Fields, April 3, 1957.
9. Justin Turner to Forest Sweet, June 4, 1957.
10. ———, "Memo for G.T.B," [1958].
11. Ironically, the Society's own files—the manuscript sources idealized by many of its members—often put the Society in a poorer light than circumstances warranted. They primarily document problems and conflicts, but not the satisfaction that many members felt with the Society's growth and the opportunities it provided for fellowship.
12. George F. Scheer's remarks, May 4, 1957.
13. Richard Maass to Walter Eastburn, July 16, 1958.

14. Richard Maass, "Notice to Dealers," March 18, 1953.

15. Mary Benjamin to David Mearns, Feb. 10, 1961.

16. Minutes, Board of Directors' meeting, Jan. 30, 1959.

CHAPTER SIX. Expanding Horizons

1. Albert B. Corey, "Rescue of Fugitive New York State Records," *Manuscripts*, Spring 1955.

2. "An Introduction to The Manuscript Society," 1959.

3. Greer Allen to the author, July 3, 1995.

4. Minutes, Board of Directors' meeting, April 11, 1964.

5. David Coblentz to Herbert Klingelhofer, April 19, 1961.

6. Unsigned article, "New York, You Were Great!," *Manuscripts,* Fall 1962.

7. Ibid.

8. Manuscript Society Press Release, Sept. 20, 1963.

9. Unsigned article, "The Generals Speak," *Manuscripts*, Summer 1964.

10. Unsigned article, "The National Convention in Washington, D.C.," *Manuscripts*, Fall 1963.

11. David Coblentz to Herbert Klingelhofer, Oct. 4, 1963.

CHAPTER SEVEN. The Winds of Change

1. Charles Hamilton, *Collecting Autographs and Manuscripts* (Norman: University of Oklahoma Press, 1961), 200–201.

2. King V. Hostick, "Record Prices," *Hobbies*, Dec. 1967.

3. Gordon T. Banks, "The Auction Market," *Manuscripts*, Summer 1965.

4. Gordon T. Banks, "What Do You Expect from an Auction House?" *Manuscripts*, Fall 1965.

5. Mary Benjamin to Stuart Schimmel, *Manuscripts*, Winter 1966.

6. Stuart B. Schimmel, "The President's Page," *Manuscripts*, Winter 1966.

7. Mary A. Benjamin, "Are Autographs an Investment?" *Hobbies*, Aug. 1966.

8. Quoted in Colton Storm, "News Notes," *Manuscripts*, Summer 1963.

9. R. M. De Shazo to Justin Turner, Sept. 4, 1964.

10. Nathaniel E. Stein, "Presidential Letters," *Manuscripts*, Fall 1965.

11. Joseph Rubinfine to the author, Oct. 26, 1995.

12. Dolly Maass to the author, Nov. 2, 1995.

13. *Kansas City Times*, Dec. 20, 1967.

14. Ellen Shaffer, "The President's Page," *Manuscripts*, Winter 1967.

15. Paul Lutz to Ellen Shaffer, Dec. 18, 1967.

16. John S. Catron to Dermot H. Stanley, Dec. 21, 1967.

17. *Kansas City Times*, Dec. 20, 1967.

18. John S. Catron to Dermot H. Stanley, Dec. 21, 1967.

19. Paul V. Lutz, "Government Loses Suit for Documents," *Manuscripts*, Fall 1967.

20. Ellen Shaffer, "The President's Page," *Manuscripts*, Fall 1967.

CHAPTER EIGHT. "A Serengeti Watering Hole"

1. David Coblentz to Herbert Klingelhofer, June 6, 1971.
2. Ellen Shaffer, "The President's Page," *Manuscripts*, Summer 1967.
3. Greer Allen to the author, July 3, 1995.
4. Ellen Shaffer, "The President's Page," *Manuscripts*, Spring 1968.
5. Paul V. Lutz, "The Autopen Dilemma," *Manuscripts*, Fall 1968.
6. Ibid.
7. Gordon Banks, "Our Shining Hour," *Manuscripts*, Spring 1971.
8. Herbert Klingelhofer to the Board of Directors [1969].
9. *Evansville* [Indiana] *Press*, Feb. 4, 1975.

CHAPTER NINE. The Harding Papers

1. Berkeley, ed., *Autographs and Manuscripts: A Collector's Manual*, 175.
2. Francis Russell, *The Shadow of Blooming Grove* (New York: McGraw-Hill, 1968), 402.
3. Russell, "The Harding Papers," *American Heritage*, Feb. 1965.
4. Ibid.
5. Kenneth Duckett to John ———— [1964].
6. Russell, *The Shadow of Blooming Grove*, ix.
7. Christie's catalogue no. 7484, May 14, 1992.
8. Paul V. Lutz, "Harding Papers Preserved," *Manuscripts*, Spring 1972.
9. Ibid.
10. Laurence C. Affron to Philip H. Jones, Dec. 1, 1991.
11. Philip H. Jones to the author, Dec. 1995.
12. News Release, College of William and Mary, Sept. 1, 1995.

CHAPTER TEN. Triumph and Disaster

1. Unsigned article, "Silver Anniversary," *Manuscripts*, Winter 1973.
2. Steve Carson to the author, Oct. 4, 1995.
3. Steve Carson to the author, Oct. 17, 1995.
4. Minutes, Board of Directors' meeting, *Manuscripts*, Winter 1973.
5. Charles Hamilton to Dewey W. Wells, March 20, 1975.
6. H. Bart Cox, "The Ownership of Public Documents," *Antiquarian Bookman*, Sept. 4, 1978.
7. Transcript by Richard Maass, quoted in *Manuscripts*, Spring 1976.
8. H. Bart Cox to the author, May 15, 1995.

9. Ibid.

10. Quoted in *Manuscripts*, Summer 1977.

11. H. Bart Cox, "More on the B.C. West Case," *The Collector*, no. 856, 1978.

12. Charles Hamilton to Dewey Wells, March 20, 1975.

13. Richard Maass, "After the B. C. West Case Decision: A Report," *Manuscripts*, Fall 1977.

14. P. W. Filby, "In Memoriam," *Manuscripts*, Summer 1977.

15. *Manuscript Society News*, Summer 1991.

CHAPTER ELEVEN. The Book

1. Herbert Klingelhofer, Memorandum to the Board of Directors, [1977].

2. Gordon T. Banks to Herbert Klingelhofer, Nov. 8, 1973.

3. Kenneth Rendell to Herbert Klingelhofer, Jan. 5, 1976.

4. Mary Benjamin to Edmund Berkeley Jr., Dec. 5, 1975.

5. Herbert Klingelhofer to Charles Cooney, Dec. 5, 1976.

6. Editor's Report to the Board of Directors, Sept. 8, 1976.

7. Ibid.

8. Kenneth Rendell to P. W. Filby, Jan. 25, 1977.

9. *New York Times*, Dec. 21, 1978.

10. *Richmond Times-Dispatch*, Jan. 14, 1979.

11. *Library Journal*, undated clipping.

12. *American Archivist*, Oct. 1979.

13. Barbara McCrimmon, "Public Apology," *Manuscripts*, Spring 1979.

CHAPTER TWELVE. Some Challenges of the 1970s

1. Minutes, Board of Directors' meeting, Jan. 24, 1976.

2. Ormonde de Kay Jr., "A Talk with Bruce Catton," *Manuscripts*, Summer 1977.

3. Charles Hamilton, "Snobbery in Autograph Collecting," *Manuscripts*, Fall 1978.

4. Minutes, Board of Directors' meeting, Oct. 28, 1978.

5. Barbara McCrimmon, "The President's Page," *Manuscripts*, Summer 1979.

6. David R. Chesnutt to the author, Sept. 1995.

7. David R. Smith to the author, Sept. 1995.

8. Robert Gordon to the author, July 6, 1995.

9. Basbanes, *A Gentle Madness*, 474.

10. Edmund Berkeley Jr., "Archivists and Thieves," *Manuscripts*, Summer 1976.

11. Kenneth W. Rendell, "Archival Security," *Manuscripts*, Winter 1977.

12. Calvin Trillin, "Knowing Johnny Jenkins," *New Yorker*, Oct. 30, 1989.

13. Ibid.

14. W. Thomas Taylor, *Texfake* (Austin: W. Thomas Taylor, 1991), 59–60.
15. Ibid.
16. Kenneth Rendell to the author, Sept. 15, 1995.
17. Michael Parrish to the author, Aug. 7, 1995.
18. *Manuscript Society News*, Spring 1990.

CHAPTER THIRTEEN. A New Constitution

1. Robert F. Batchelder, "The Market," *Manuscripts*, Fall 1979.
2. Wilmer S. Roberts, "The Private Collector and Inflation," *Manuscripts*, Fall 1979.
3. Winston Broadfoot, "How Inflation Affects Institutional Collecting," *Manuscripts*, Fall 1979.
4. Robert McCown, "The New Orleans Annual Meeting," *Manuscripts*, Fall 1979.
5. Howard Applegate, Memorandum to the Board, March 31, 1980.
6. *Manuscript Society News*, Fall 1980.
7. *Manuscript Society News*, Summer 1981.
8. Syd Cauveren to the author, March 10, 1995.
9. *Manuscript Society News*, Summer 1982.
10. Ibid.

CHAPTER FOURTEEN. The Life Member

1. Charles Hamilton, *Great Forgers and Famous Fakes* (New York: Crown, 1980), 158.
2. Robert A. Jones, "The White Salamander Murders," *Los Angeles Times Magazine*, March 29, 1987.
3. Robert Lindsey, *A Gathering of Saints* (New York: Simon & Schuster, 1988), 154.
4. Ibid., 156.
5. Kenneth W. Rendell, "Latter Day Taints: The Mark Hofmann Case," *Manuscripts*, Winter 1988.
6. Lindsey, *A Gathering of Saints*, 351.
7. Ibid., 373.
8. Jones, "The White Salamander Murders," *Los Angeles Times Magazine*, March 29, 1987.
9. Kenneth W. Rendell, *Forging History* (Norman: University of Oklahoma Press, 1994), 126.
10. Ibid., 125.
11. Ibid., 371.
12. *Manuscript Society Newsletter*, Winter 1988.

CHAPTER FIFTEEN. New Fields

1. *Manuscript Society News*, Summer 1985.

2. Ibid., Summer 1984.

3. Ibid., Summer 1985.

4. Ira Brilliant to the author, Oct. 17, 1995.

5. Ira Brilliant to the author, Dec. 1995.

6. Ira Brilliant, "Information Exchange Database Opens at Arizona State University," *Manuscripts*, Winter 1990.

7. Barbara L. Neilon writing in *Journal of Academic Librarianship*, Nov. 1985.

8. Minutes, Board of Trustees' meeting, Oct. 18, 1986.

9. *Manuscript Society News*, Summer 1987.

CHAPTER SIXTEEN. The Society in the 1990s

1. Minutes, Board of Trustees' meeting, Oct. 27, 1990.

2. *Wall Street Journal*, July 6, 1990.

3. Ibid.

4. Information on this Turner-Manarin controversy is derived largely from an article by Turner in the May 12, 1986, issue of *Antiquarian Bookman*.

5. Bill Turner to the author, Dec. 22, 1995.

6. Bill Turner, "Replevin," *Manuscripts*, Fall 1986.

7. Ibid.

8. *Norfolk Virginian-Pilot*, April 3, 1992.

9. Jack D. Hamilton, statement, Feb. 15, 1991.

10. *Richmond Times-Dispatch*, Feb. 27, 1991.

11. Williamsburg Circuit Court, Chancery No. 8510, Discovery Deposition of Dr. Louis Henry Manarin, April 30, 1991, pp. 6–7.

12. *Memorandum of Amicus Curiae—The Manuscript Society*, May 15, 1991.

13. Scott W. Petersen, "Replevin: Are Your Documents Safe?" *Manuscripts*, Fall 1993.

14. *Norfolk Virginian-Pilot*, April 3, 1992.

CHAPTER SEVENTEEN. Word Shadows of the Great

1. *Civilization*, May/June 1995, 43.

2. Leon Harris, "Signed, Dealed and Delivered," *Town & Country*, Feb. 1990.

3. William R. Coleman to the author, Oct. 20, 1995.

4. Herbert Klingelhofer to the author, March 1996.

5. Madeleine Stern to the author, Oct. 19, 1995.

6. Ibid.

7. Harris, "Signed, Dealed and Delivered."

8. Joseph Rubinfine to the author, Oct. 26, 1995.

9. Basbanes, *A Gentle Madness*, 438.

10. Ibid., 437.

11. Stephen Bumball, "A Document Returns After 42 Years," *Manuscripts*, Summer 1988.

12. *Manuscript Society News*, Winter 1991.

13. *Wall Street Journal*, May 15, 1981.

14. Richard Maass, "The Gettysburg Address We Lost," *Manuscripts*, Spring 1982.

15. Albert H. Small to the author, April 9, 1996.

16. *Manuscript Society News*, Winter 1996.

Recommended Reading

Benjamin, Mary A. *Autographs: A Key to Collecting*. New York: R. R. Bowker, 1946; rev. ed., 1963. One of the first books on autographs, by a prominent dealer.

Berkeley, Edmund, Jr., ed. *Autographs and Manuscripts: A Collector's Manual*. New York: Charles Scribner's Sons, 1978. Perhaps the most comprehensive reference book on autograph collecting, published by the Manuscript Society.

Cahoon, Herbert, Thomas V. Lange, and Charles Ryskamp, eds. *American Literary Autographs*. New York: Dover, 1977. A profusely illustrated volume, published in collaboration with the Morgan Library.

Hamilton, Charles. *Collecting Autographs and Manuscripts*. Norman: University of Oklahoma Press, 1961; rev. ed., Modoc Press, 1963. Probably the best single introduction to autographs.

_____ . *The Robot That Helped to Make a President*. New York: Author, 1965. Although other dealers had become suspicious of JFK autographs, this book explained about the Autopen.

_____ . *The Signature of America*. New York: Harper & Row, 1979. A useful volume on American autographs, with many facsimiles.

_____ . *Great Forgers and Famous Fakes*. New York: Crown, 1980. An anecdotal guide to some famous forgers.

_____ . *American Autographs*. 2 vols. Norman: University of Oklahoma Press, 1983. A comprehensive guide, copiously illustrated.

Harris, Robert. *Selling Hitler*. London: Faber and Faber, 1986. A detailed history of the Hitler diaries caper.

Madigan, Thomas F. *Word Shadows of the Great*. New York: Frederick A. Stokes, 1930. An early work, attractively written but hard to find.

Nickell, Joe. *Pen, Ink & Evidence*. Lexington: University Press of Kentucky, 1990. A profusely illustrated history of writing materials in court cases.

Rawlins, Ray. *The Stein and Day Book of World Autographs*. New York: Stein and Day, 1978. Brief descriptions of notables and their autographs, emphasizing European material and the arts.

Rendell, Kenneth W. *Forging History*. Norman: University of Oklahoma Press, 1994. An interesting and attractive discussion of forgeries, with emphasis on the technical means of their detection.

Reese, Michael II. *Autographs of the Confederacy*. New York: Cohasco, Inc., 1981. Examples of the signatures of almost all prominent Confederates.

Taylor, John M. *From the White House Inkwell*. Rutland, Vt.: Charles E. Tuttle, 1968; rev. ed., Modoc Press, 1989. The first book on a specialized area of autograph collecting—American Presidents.

———, ed. *Autograph Collector's Checklist*. Burbank, Calif.: 1990. A research aid sponsored by the Manuscript Society, briefly noting the rarity of various autographs.

Taylor, Priscilla S., ed. *Manuscripts: The First Twenty Years*. Westport, Conn.: Greenwood Press, 1984. An anthology of the best articles from the early journals of the Manuscript Society.

Index

About the Author

JOHN M. TAYLOR graduated from Williams College in 1952 with honors in history, and earned a master's degree from George Washington University in 1954. From 1952 until 1987 he was employed by the U.S. government, in agencies concerned with intelligence and foreign affairs.

A past president and a fellow of the Manuscript Society, Mr. Taylor is the author of seven books in history and biography. His most recent biography, *Confederate Raider: Raphael Semmes of the Alabama*, was a 1995 selection of the History Book Club. His immediately previous work was another biography, *William Henry Seward: Lincoln's Right Hand* (1991; paperback, 1997).

Mr. Taylor's earlier works include a biography of his father, *General Maxwell Taylor: The Sword and the Pen* (1989; paperback, 1990) and a book about presidential autographs, *From the White House Inkwell* (1970, rev. ed., 1989). He is a frequent contributor to historical magazines. A collection of his Civil War articles, *While Cannons Roared*, was published in mid-1997.

ISBN 0-275-95918-X

EAN

90000>

9 780275 959180

HARDCOVER BAR CODE